Who's Who in *Vermont Odysseys*

State Rep. Bill Mares covers the legislature, an old-fashioned body dealing with modern issues.

Norman Runnion, Brattleboro *Reformer* editor for twenty years, reports on the battle beween the natives and the Flatlanders.

Frank Bryan, of *The Vermont Papers* and *Real Vermonters Don't Milk Goats,* contributes a moving portrait of native Vermonter Bucky Cole, whose hobby is raising oxen and whose dignity is being denied.

Norma Skjold, a young widow who finds in a year of losses that the cutting down of the stately roadside trees in front of her home is the final heartbreak.

. . . And 12 more outspoken, heartfelt voices of new and old Vermonters about the state they love.

C. L. Gilbert is a freelance writer and editor who lives in Montpelier, Vermont.

For Martin, one of life's better editors

Contents

Introduction

As I write this, it is eighteen below zero, extending the coldest December in record around here. My truck battery is warming by the wood stove and a pan of coals glows under the oil pan outside. Last night I came home after two days away. My cabin, usually tight and snug, had succumbed to the brutal cold and the faucets were frozen. Fortunately, the basement, insulated by the earth around, had stayed warm enough to keep the pipes below from freezing. Another day away, however, and I would have had big problems.

I fired up the wood stove, put the cookstove on broil, and opened the door. I lit the gas heater in the basement, set the electric space heater in the bathroom, and began massaging the pipes under the sink lightly with a propane torch. I also melted snow on the wood stove, poured the heated water into mason jars, and set them into my tropical fish tank, whose little submersible heater had been unable to keep up with the cold and had allowed the water to cool to an untropical sixty-two degrees.

A passing irritation and all is well now. The exercise in converting water from a solid to a liquid state is merely one of those things one deals with as a matter of course in Vermont—that is, if you are foolish enough to leave your house unheated and unattended in a record-setting December. Outside my window now, the chickadees and blue jays have come to check the feeder to see what I've left them. In this weather, just about any crust of bread seems to excite them. They are my only wild visitors in winter and have become friendly as dogs.

I take note of these things hoping the facts will lend themselves to some kind of metaphorical insight into what Vermont is all about, as if the cold and the birds and the wood stove are important pieces in the search for a definition of this place. I suppose they are, but I struggle to figure out the connection—and to extend that—to figure out what the universal experience of freezing pipes and endless arm loads of firewood imprints upon the other inhabitants of this wonderful little place and thus collectively draws us together.

I could, I suppose, turn to the theory that we live closer to nature, are more in touch with the turning of the seasons and the vagaries of the weather, and we glory in the small things around us that are missing from lives led in more hectic and civilized places. These things, the theory goes, have helped cast the Vermont character, which is said to be tough, independent, taciturn, and self-reliant. Descriptors such as "flinty" and "feisty" often get thrown into such definitions.

Maybe. Of course, as much as we like to think it is so, we are not unique in many of these things. There are batteries warming by wood stoves in North Dakota, after all, and folks in Florida keep as close track of the birds in their yards as we. Family farms have been passed through the generations in every state, and isolation has created both inventiveness and backwardness in, say, Texas, as much as it has in Vermont. So perhaps the answer lies elsewhere, in the sense of history, the New England tradition, the smallness, the sense of community, the sense that one can manage here because the scale of life is human-sized.

I can accept that, I think, because those are some of the reasons I like being here. (It isn't for the skiing or the fishing or the agricultural opportunities, all of which—despite claims to the contrary—are better elsewhere.) But still, Vermonters, in the most important ways, are pretty much like people most other places. They are forward-thinking and bigoted and honest and cowardly and caring of others and selfish. They respect the earth and they pollute it, they rejoice in simple things and complicate their lives with trivia. They love their children and they beat them, conceive, love, and die in the same manner as all humankind. The similarities with others are, for the most part, greater than the differences.

Vermont Odysseys

But no, many will protest. There is something. Vermonters are different and the state itself is different. It is our bicentennial year in 1991, and we will hear a great deal about this state and what makes it one of a kind. And it will be hard to argue that we are special and blessed in ways that our friends just east of the Connecticut River or west of Lake Champlain and those north and south of our borders are not. We will have to fight the urge to translate different to mean better, but, of course, that is what we mean.

I have tried to put my finger on the difference and come up empty-handed, short of clichés. Driving from New Hampshire back to Vermont, I am always struck by what happens when crossing the Connecticut River. There seems to be a moment when I relax suddenly, as if I've escaped. Maybe I'm just glad to be getting home, the horse smelling the barn and all, but something inside rejects this rationality saying there is a spirit in the graspable contours of the landscape and the knots of humanity tucked in between the folds of the hills and embodied in the sight of the rising church steeple, the working farm, and the sawmill. There is something that these tangible things create that produce this intangible feeling I get, but I've yet to hear anyone satisfactorily encase it in words.

Which gets back to the people included in this book. They are Vermonters all, to one degree or another. Some are natives, some are not. The years spent do not seem to me as important as the insight gained and then articulated.

There is, of course, the classic tale of the flatlander who, having lived in Vermont for twenty years, asks a native why it is that the townsfolk still don't consider him as one of them. After a moment of thought, the native says, "Well if you had a cat, and the cat crawled in the oven, and the cat had kittens, t'wouldn't be muffins."

I've always admired the clean logic of that story but have trouble making the leap from cats to people. These days, I'm not so sure most people would demand such a rigorous heritage to be considered a Vermonter simply because most people are from somewhere else. The ranks of the born-and-bred have been seriously thinned by the moved-here-recently. There is a great deal of sadness and anguish over this influx of bodies. In fact, in these pages, more than one writer reflects on the implications of this immigration. Crime, condos, highways, pollution, budget deficits, it's all here now, and it is difficult to accept, especially when contemplating the way things used to be.

Sixteen writers have contributed to this collection, and their work is as eclectic as they are—as Vermont is. Through their eyes we get glimpses of the past and visions of the future.

Rickey Gard Diamond, in "The Longest Shortcut," takes us on a trip down a back road, one whose wanderings provide insight into not only geography but place; Norma Skjold shares the anguish at losing control over her property in her touching "On Straightening a Curve in the Road," which serves as a metaphor for personal loss; in "On Main Street, It's Raining," Doug Wilhelm describes the attraction of Vermont and why wanderers find this a good place to stop, even if for a little while.

Several essays give us an uncompromising look at the impact of development on Vermont, one of the state's most pressing issues. Norman Runnion in "The Gentrification of Vermont," Lennie Britton in "They No Longer Play Softball on Main Street," and Frank Bryan in "We Are All Farmers" all force us to examine the way the state is growing, how it affects families, and why the emphasis on the value of the individual is as important today as it was a century ago.

Art and inspiration are discussed from different perspectives. Tom Slayton's "Sacred Harp" looks at the archetypes behind a unique Vermont art form, one originating here, while Andy Potok, in "Foliage Season," reflects on a much different source of his artistic motivation.

In "A Cabinet of Curiosities," Joe Citro gives us a dark look behind the church steeples and leafy hills, a look that undermines our stereotypes; Geof Hewitt recalls the trying and hilarious idealism of the sixties back-to-the-land movement in "To Hell with the Homestead!"; and Alex Wilson, in "Midmorning Break," points the way to environmentally sound building practices while searching for balance in life. Can a square peg fit in a round hole? Bill Mares tries to in "An Outsider's Inside View of the Legislature"; and Lee Huntington in "Aged in Vermont" discusses the virtues of growing old in Vermont—no Florida sunshine for her. Family trust is the theme of the sailing saga "The First Lesson" by Fred Stetson; in "Water" by Howard Norman, family takes on a different meaning; and, finally, in "The Things We Do for Lamb," Don Mitchell provides a humorous and tender look at the joys and dangers of raising sheep.

Vermont Odysseys is a compass that swings wildly in every direction. Which is the point. It does not lead to a neat conclusion, there is no destination at the end. If there is a moral to its story, I suppose it would be that Vermont is a state with as many legitimate definitions as there are inhabitants. With sixteen of those definitions presented here, the surface of our understanding has just been scratched.

As for me, such musings have to be put aside; I've got to get the steps shoveled and the week's wood brought inside.

—*C.L. Gilbert*

The Longest Shortcut

Rickey Gard Diamond

We had a business date, and it was odd, his standing me up. Not like him to miss an appointment. And then an hour after we were to meet for lunch I got a call: "You're probably not going to believe this," he said. "I got lost somewhere between Waterbury and Barre."

These two towns are practically in our backyard. He was right, it did seem like nonsense. But I did believe him.

Earlier that week I had decided to take a shortcut myself, following directions that another friend had suggested, "up past the cemetery, right over the hill." This would take me the back way from Barre to Plainfield, an area I generally know quite well. In fact, the minute my friend described the route to me, I realized how silly it had been, all those trips the way I usually went — the way the zigzag routes you drive in Vermont often seem silly — going round the mountain by driving first northwest on Route 14, then roundabout east on Route 2.

So I set out over the hills toward Plainfield on a straightforward path, knowing it was, well, not far and about over there. Up past the new split-level ranch-style homes of the granite industry executives with their acres of lawn I drove. Up farther, past a few old Capes restored with paints in colors our ancestors would never have dreamed of, their rock walls rebuilt, grass clipped short without benefit of sheep, and up deeper still into the mountain, to where my friend had told me the asphalt would end. The gravel sent a spray of tiny stones against my car, hissing and pinging.

7

One thing my friend had failed to mention, and that was the fork, a very narrow fork so that it was hard to say which way for sure. . . .

But I chose, still looking toward the general direction of Plainfield, which lay about over there, the other side of that hill. Feeling confident still. Because, generally, I knew my way around.

And then, as roads will do in Vermont, the route began to narrow, its dirt edges crumbled by the trickle of water that follows, or rather leads, most mountain roads in directions all twisty and loopy. It followed its own secret inclinations, not human logic. And the houses here, I noticed, were farther between, untouched by paint, leaning from the weight of so many years, and the trees were coming close, pushing in against the roofs and the roadside.

In the yards of these houses and on their porches and setting up against the outside walls were piles of weathered lumber and window frames and metal bedsprings, yes, and washing machines and crates and crates of—stuff. Clearly these folks did not believe in the careless ways of consumerism; they were Saving for A Rainy Day, clinging to the humbler, older virtue of thrift. Ancient cars hunkered down in the tall grass of their yards, nearly overgrown, except for the ones that were set up on cement blocks, Frankensteins waiting for some lightning bolt of resurrection. Huge, sad-eyed dogs watched me pass, their silence ominous.

I traveled for what seemed a very long time, then doubled back and tried the fork not taken. Sheer obstinacy made me prevail when that one, too, seemed to change its mind and be going in directions opposite to Plainfield or, possibly, to anywhere else I decided I wanted to go.

Vermont back roads can be treacherous that way. And they all look deceptively alike. The houses on the south fork look amazingly like the north fork, and the route begins to even remind you of some road you saw—you swear it—in another county, Rutland maybe, or Caledonia, far to the south or the north from here, but by that time, you fear you're hallucinating.

Back roads stamp you as the intruder you are, a city mouse used to road signs and straight demarcations laid out in a sensible grid pattern. Here the roads follow the instinctive direction of creeks and gullies, following their own pace, wending themselves down a hill by the natural lay of the land, past rocks that must have been pushed here by monstrous forces—millions of years before there were vertebrates, much less the likes of a hairless mammal like you. You had forgotten all that, if you ever thought about it at all. Here, you compare yourself to the land and understand your species not to be entirely in charge.

When you stop at a house finally, where you see people out in the yard, their faces clearly show just how foreign you are. It doesn't help that you know in the larger picture of American society, these Vermonters are the peculiar ones. Here, on the back roads, you are the one in trouble.

Or maybe not in such trouble actually. Just bear on this road for another mile and a half and Plainfield would be to your left, the natives told me. I came out about eight miles above where I'd planned to, a good twenty miles above where I usually came out on Route 14, but the sight of that paved road and the broader, stony creek that led to it—a slightly less tortured path—was a blessed sight, and the feel of that smooth road under my tires, soothing. Where a moment before I'd felt anxiety and frustration, I now felt elation. And I was lucky. I didn't have someone waiting for me that I'd have to phone and 'fess up to, shamefaced: You won't believe this, but I got lost between Barre and Plainfield. If I had, though, it's likely the person on the other end, if he or she had done any traveling in the state, would understand and forgive, knowing it would be just a matter of time before it happened to them again.

Today's modern roads are not meant to elicit any such toleration of imperfection. They are designed by high-paid engineers who follow exact and documented standards aimed at straightening the way and smoothing it, shooting us down the highway of life, if you're lucky, like the radio sings, in a pink Cadillac. Roads are intended to be no more than a means to an end, and modern highways announce their well-lit intentions on reflective signs, their splits and forks clearly labeled—most of the time—and maneuvered with hardly a reduction in speed and certainly without the wait of an intersection. Zoom, one goes under; roar, the other curves over, and off you go, your taillights red and merging into the sunset on the horizon. Or so it goes in the car commercials.

During rush hour, coming into a strange city, you can, of course, feel all sorts of emotions traveling on newly revised roads, but these will soon pass. Your not yet being a well-trained rat in this particular maze temporarily overshadows the more direct intention of getting you around quickly with the least interference possible. A few times of getting from here to there and you'll have the route and its ensuing pressures down to a science, too.

In fact, the real problem comes from being joined by so many other human beings also intending to get there quickly with the least possible interference, and they all know the road better and drive faster and give you dirty looks for their having to pass you because you are going 4 MPH slower than they are. The trouble comes from the traffic and the predictable anomalies of human nature, not from the roads themselves, which are state-of-the-art and straightish and undisturbed by stops and starts and unmarked forks.

Feelings in such a setting are distinctly different than those elicited by being lost on a Vermont back road, which, depending upon how long you've been lost, tend to echo hollowly in your solitary breast, somewhat like a heron landing in a pond and stalking round the edges, occasionally stabbing with his beak at a likely prospect. This way? Over here?

Being lost on a superhighway in the city feels more like a whole flock of pigeons panicked into flight, rising in a wave of wings that ripples alarmingly this way, then that. Then, safe, finding your well-marked exit, usually within a matter of minutes (though it can seem longer), anxiety's flock lands rather abruptly and, shrugging its wings into order, begins cooing and strutting, self-congratulatory at making such good time, after all. There are only two superhighways in Vermont, I-89 and I-91, and, like me, they are relative newcomers. Both are simple, straightforward affairs as such highways go, stretching vertically through our longish state on either side of its mountainous backbone. Only in White River Junction where the two highways briefly touch do you have the sort of bewildering and disorienting cloverleaf exits in directions opposite to where you are headed, such as are common elsewhere. But even these are well marked and relatively simple and all that there are on these otherwise straight ribbons of road.

Both highways stretch high and yield views that are beautiful no matter what the season: the white and many blues of winter; the chartreuse of spring buds and full-blown green chenille of leafy summer; or, most famous of all, the scarlet and orange and yellow of autumn, which blends on the far hills to a hazy purple. Looking down, you can see villages clustered around bends in a river, white church steeples, red barns, and rock-wall-edged fields. It stirs nostalgia in those who travel here, and thanks to the superhighways, more and more people do. As someone once said, Vermont is our collective past, what we all used to be, and we all feel a kind of connection to it.

If you are truly interested in the past, though, you can see back even farther than early American days, because of the blasting of road engineers seeking to make those roads straight and convenient and conducive to the higher speeds that are the standard today. Great walls of rock have been sheared out of the mountains in places—a geologist's dream—the rocks' striations evidence of past time in comparison to which we humans are mere fractions of a second. And what powers have been locked into the foundations of this state!

The Green Mountains, which travel from the southern end of Vermont to the Canadian border, have at their core the oldest kind of Precambrian rock, a good four-and-a-half-billion years old, covered with younger, metamorphosed rock that was upfolded by the pressure of two tectonic plates squeezing in together. Ancient sediment and volcanic lava were laid down in horizontal layers, but you can see in the rock cuts how the layers have been compressed and folded into what geologists call anticlines and thrust faults, its clays and glacial flours cooked into quartz and marble and garnet in the process.

The Precambrian rock has been shoved up to the surface in places because of this folding action. During the Acadian mountain-building period, according to the geologic interpretation that is now most accepted, New Hampshire was a piece of Africa or Europe, which explains once and for all the differences between the two states celebrated everywhere in Vermont. But it was this continental collision and the resulting pressure inland that convoluted slices of Vermont rock and formed the Green

Mountains down its middle, and ever since, the Green Mountains have been dominating everything around these parts, not least of all the human beings who eventually settled on their slopes.

Some say the people took the character of the granite right up through the soles of their feet. They got craggy as the mountains and even their voices took on a hard-edged nasally twang, the famous Yankee speech that for the most part was silent as the rocks around them.

This character shaping happened only when the same kind of pressure that shaped the mountains happened on a more human level. When the more desirable bottomlands were used up and stony mountain ground was the only acreage a body could afford, that's when Vermont got settled and all those rock walls got built. And people stayed, generally only if they did not have other choices. Just as millions of years before, the continents of Europe and Africa decided to head elsewhere and the mountains were left alone; when the industrial age opened up whole new careers in the 1830s, then all but the hardiest people ebbed to easier, lower terrain.

Now pressure is building again.

The hardwood forests of New Jersey and Connecticut and most of the nation are long, long gone, first to rich farms, then to industry, and, now in the era of the service economy, to 7-Elevens. There is very little left that is quaint or down-country in such a terrain.

I used to think Vermont really was a special, different sort of place. Now I think it's just behind the times. We have the mountains to be grateful to for that, their inherent difficulty having blocked development and saved this place for last. Vermont is behind everybody's time—the reason so many people love it. Who doesn't like to go back for a visit to simpler, quieter places? For generations, Vermonters lived rustic lives because they had no choice. But even people from New Jersey can put up with the inconvenience if it's just for a lark. The problem is some of us like it so much we struggle to live here year-round. Some of us struggle to keep it behind the times.

There's an innate hypocrisy to that stance that sneaks up on you while you're on the soapbox, of course. Everybody's anti-development mood comes upon them suddenly just after they've got their place all situated. Okay. Now I'm settled. Let's keep this place just as it is.

That people have a right to live freely in this country is what our own Green Mountain Boys fought for. Ira and Ethan Allen wanted their place all situated, just like you and I got ours. My own ancestors moved out to the Northwest Territory, themselves armed with the same philosophy. They'd heard the lands were flat and rich, and folks like mine, without easier choices, could at least build a raft and float their belongings down the Ohio River, traveling through land without any roads at all, just Indian trails. It was in this wild territory, about the time that people began ebbing out of Vermont the first time, that one of my forefathers, Josephus Gard, met up with and married Laura Farley. Her people originally came from Vermont.

President Andrew Jackson gave a land grant to the Gards in exchange for hogs supplied to his army, though I'm not certain where in the territory this was. Ten Gard brothers had tried Ohio first, then southern Indiana, and finally, hearing of more opportunities, some headed north, up the Michigan trail. They withstood the angry objections of the Iroquois, who had considered this their hunting land, by holing up at Fort Miami, named for the Indians who had lived there before the Iroquois ran them off.

Josephus, once he was finished with chasing after the gold rush, leaving poor Laura behind, settled in southwestern Michigan because of the oak trees. Having come back from the gold fields of California empty-handed except for a new skill in the leather business, he needed their leaves for his tanning vats.

Josephus's farmland ran east from Lake Michigan to the St. Joseph River, high enough to escape the earliest killing frosts. For over a hundred years the Gards grew apples and grapes there, plums and peaches. That is, until my own grandfather found, as is happening in Vermont today, that taxes made farming less profitable than selling off the land.

Piece by little piece, he sold it. When I left my home state in 1980 to settle in Vermont, my grandparents' big farmhouse had a McDonald's in the front yard and an IGA supermarket off the side porch. Its hand-hewn barn, joists bound together with rawhide strips and wooden pegs, had earned a feature story in the local paper before it was torn down, but no Gards lived in the county any longer. The homestead had been split into apartments, dividing the living room, where my grandmother had taught me hymns at the piano, from the library, where my grandfather indulged me with play on his old black Remington typewriter, used by him to write poetry and letters to *The Atlantic Monthly*. Across the road and down to the river, where my father used to take me hiking, were regiments of neat, brick homes — upscale from the Gard farmhouse, every one.

Last year, I heard they moved the old house where once a half-dozen grandkids had raced round the two staircases, impatient for dinner to begin, to sit on a quieter road named for our family; someone converted the place to a bed and breakfast. I hear it's a going concern. The house is probably cleaner and lovelier, more luxurious and polished than it had ever been the whole while that generations of Gards stored crates of apples in the root cellar. And I can't stand the thought.

When I go to South Burlington now, all this comes to mind. I lose heart, like my grandfather must have, being shaped by what everybody else seems to want — certainly nothing so simple as a well-grown apple or a skillfully crafted sentence. It's like bracing yourself against a tectonic plate that carries a continent. Even if you are rock, it will fold you like a fan.

When I am feeling Romantic, in the best, most traditional sense of that word, I imagine myself come back to reclaim what my Farley foremother left. I am bent on building a life that is simpler and closer to the land, though my efforts are uneven and my lifestyle inconsistent. I buy 100 percent organic vitamins, from A to E, and store them in bottles in a drawer. Knowing what's good for me doesn't always translate into action.

The first time I saw Vermont was through tinted glass from the high-perched seat of a bus on my way to Goddard College from Michigan by way of I-89. By that time I had been sitting upright, squeezed in upon by strangers, for about twenty-one hours. Vermont still touched me; I sat up a little straighter, paid closer attention. There were those dramatic rock outcroppings next to the highway and that open span of Lake Champlain, spread, it seemed, with silver, and as we drove into the heart of the state, mountains and views such as no midwesterner would dream existed outside of *National Geographic.* From the beginning I believed the sight of so much green was feeding me, and by the time the bus reached Waterbury, I was scheming to somehow move here.

Thousands of people have fled the cities and suburbs to come here as I did and pretend to be country people and, in some cases, to actually become country people. There are giveaways of the first group, like Birkenstock sandals that no native would be caught dead in and a certain liberal squeamishness about hunting and killing livestock that tends to be the product of privileged lives. For the most part, though, this group's values seek to preserve the life-style of the sturdier native stock who, by and large, are not so enamored of Vermont's nonexistent good old days as they are by its increasing value in the country's real estate market. Therein is the present tension in Vermont politics. Back roads do get you lost, but they can also get you away from the hustle that comes with a modern I-89. They can help you see the possibility of another way of getting from here to there, a more interesting way maybe, certainly a more beautiful way. It might take more time even when you think it's a shortcut, it could be downright dangerous if the wrong kind of weather blows up, but it's a different way than we are used to and a way that also rings some remote inner bells.

I've found people on these roads who have not completely forgotten the cycles of the earth that underlie everything. Most often necessity dictates this faithfulness, but here and there, you find people who have chosen to stay connected despite having other choices. They've taken the longest shortcut of all to get here, like Moses' people, through years of wandering the wilderness of city streets, moving in and out of desolate suburbs.

Some of these people question if we're really so entitled to the soft, easy life that an ever-expanding economy has promised us. They don't even so much believe in the limitless bounty and forgiveness of nature anymore—and they're wondering, how come we think we're the big exception to what all life has always struggled for with such difficulty: survival. That we have any choice other than to understand and live with the earth's cycles that underlie everything may be the most dangerous delusion of all those our civilization indulges.

Even when the understanding of this is only intuitive and held within a limited perspective, folks on back roads who still know how to hunt and trap and where to find the best berries and fiddleheads are at a distinct advantage. They know wood ash and manure is good for the garden. They understand the difference between soil and dirt. They kill hens that are done with their laying and don't blink an eye sitting down to eat chicken and biscuits. They tend not to be shaken by much and are even less likely to be impressed.

Call it a sense of perspective. Cyanobacteria, the first community of life on earth, that proverbial primordial slime, ruled the planet for a good three-and-a-half billion years before it did itself in with pollution. It thrived in the carbon dioxide atmosphere that first surrounded our planet, for eons carelessly chugging out a noxious, gaseous by-product—oxygen—which, as it turns out, was essential for up-and-coming animal life but deadly for that first golden age. And the rock at the heart of our mountains was already there, witness to this earliest rise and fall.

That gives me hope that even if we screw up the ozone and make our environment unfit for human habitation, other life-forms will take our place, maybe life that thrives on acid rain and toxic waste. The mountains attest that this is possible; at the same time they warn us that no species is wise to believe itself safe, not when you've ruled for three-and-a-half billion years, not even when you've ushered in the age of technology and better living through chemistry. Devastation and suffering are nothing; the only thing that nature abhors is a vacuum.

I am always pleased when I come to Hill Harvest Farm just as the cows are crossing the back road I take from Montpelier into Barre. Then I have to stop and wait for them and am late for whatever appointment I have, but I don't care if I make whomever I'm meeting with cranky. It's a wonderful excuse I'd dare anyone to argue with—but the cows were crossing! And they took their sweet time. And they looked at me with those steady, soulful eyes that were—yes!—contented.

This morning the farm woman who always opens the gate for them called to them to hurry up. She came over to the car because I had wound my window down. Before, whenever I've passed this way or stopped for the cows, I've waved at her but she's always looked surprised, unsure of who I was, maybe uncertain as to how to respond to a woman who wears earrings first off in the morning. I was pleased she felt friendly enough to come over and talk, a benchmark in my years traveling this road.

What kind of car was this I was driving, she started off. A Honda, I answered. What kind of cows are those? Turns out they are Ayrshires, registered ones. Lady Ripple there is the selfsame cow that was on the statehouse lawn just a few weeks ago, she told me, with 2,000 schoolkids and all of them wanting to milk her. Yes, ole Ripple came back and laid herself down for the rest of the day and couldn't even say what for!

By then the last of Lady Ripple's bovine companions were across the road and headed down the path the cows had worn wide on their way to pasture. I said good-bye and set out to finish my own morning trek, my schedule a little late, but my inclination to always take this roundabout route made stronger now that I had something close to neighbors on this road.

Actually, I won't always take this route, much as I love it; I'll take it only in good weather. Back roads don't just demand that you know them firsthand but that you pay attention and not take safety for granted. The same road I was so relieved to come out on in Plainfield after I was lost in the hills on my way from Barre was washed away just a few weeks later by floodwaters rushing down the mountain after a heavy rainstorm, carrying a house away with a massive chunk of the road. This kind of disaster, too, is part of the scenery.

I used to take the road past the Hill Harvest Farm absolutely every day until the second cold, snowy day of my first winter on the hill. The very first cold, snowy day I asked myself, coming home, would it be smart to come down the hill? Had the snowplow taken care of things for me? In a hurry, I decided to chance it.

The road coming down our side of the mountain faces the east, so snow really wasn't a problem. The sun had melted everything; in fact, streams of water must have gone coursing down along the road in the full sunshine earlier that day because by the time I came down, the sun was gone, the water was frozen, and in the snow's place were patches of ice as smooth as any ice-skating rink's. Now the trouble is that once you've made the decision to head down, and you find yourself sliding in a direction that you suddenly notice has no relationship to the direction in which you have just turned your steering wheel—when that happens—it's too late. You have nothing to do then except concentrate on creative wheel turning, pumping your brakes lightly on those places where it appears the gravel is clear so as to staunch the increasing pressure of your velocity.

It is absolutely true that everything gets heavier on the downside of a mountain in winter, perhaps the result of congealed ice crystals, maybe the barometric pressure—whatever the scientific cause, all is heavy: the breath held taut in your lungs, your heartbeat, the weight of your muscles, your eyes popping out from all that tonnage of terror squeezing, as downward you lunge.

There are far worse close calls that Vermonters on winter roads have survived and lived to tell the tale about. And worse stories still about getting around in mud season—what the uninitiated blithely call "spring." One thing you can say, and often will say the minute you get together with others to swap stories about frost heaves and washboard hills—eager to laugh and compensate for those other stories you know that didn't end so well, those deadly curves and bad weather that killed—any such lesson learned on a back road tends to stick with you. I, for one, will never again be oblivious to cold days and their horrifying possibilities on mountainsides.

On the other hand, I will still risk mud season on slightly gooey roads for the sight of a broad span of new green and burgundy on spring maple saplings. That's because, being downhome, old-fashioned kinds of places, why naturally, back roads teach you in homilies, not in standardized theories or accepted practices and procedures. Homilies quite frequently end up being entirely opposite, like the forks you find en route and the shortcuts that take whole afternoons. Look Before You Leap, they say, and on the other hand, She Who Hesitates Is Lost. No signposts here, just the chance to test the trustworthiness of your instincts and the certainty of consequences for whatever choices you make.

With any luck, you'll meet up with folks who don't much like the main road either, who may even be able to give you directions home. And the mountains will be your witness.

On Main Street, It's Raining

Douglas Wilhelm

I came to Vermont from New Jersey, by way of Kathmandu.

I was a sort of refugee. I'd been covering ground in the uneasy way that you'll see among some people who've had a good education, and every opportunity, in the Western world. I was not sure where or what my oppression was but kept my distance from it anyway. I needed a place where I could do work that was my own. I came to Vermont with a hangover and haven't left.

Yesterday I was reading some magazine articles about how more Americans are valuing small places again, small towns and onetime hardscrabble hill farms with gnarly old apple trees where the people put in new kitchens and, if they are writers, go on to tell us about their woodpile, the setbacks that brought them wisdom as they tended their first pickle crop, that gnarly apple tree. I would like, sometimes, to be living that well-grounded a life. But I got damn tired, last winter, of hacking at the ice-locked woodpile at the little schoolhouse in the country where my wife and little boy live. I never made any pickles, and in March I moved into town. Into Montpelier, the small capital city where I work and where I seem to know everybody—I walk the streets waving to people and stopping to talk, like some visiting diplomat. It's a good town and Vermont is a very good place, but on this rainy spring morning I think I am still a kind of refugee. I will stay here, but even so.

I grew up in New Jersey, though I wasn't born there. Very few people who live in the New Jersey suburbs (or any other suburbs) were born there, and not too many people who live up here were born in Vermont, either. Not anymore. It's a displaced society, a disconnected world.

But to try and wrestle some narrative into this: I worked in New Jersey, through most of my twenties, on weekly newspapers in the suburbs while I lived in an outlying town, Long Valley, on a farm that was auctioned off while we were there. We shared a small house in the barnyard, myself and my sister, who is a muralist—I remember half a dozen plywood panels painted with an African savannah scene spread across the New Jersey grass— her then-husband, who played bass guitar in a bar band called the Blue Sparks From Hell; and an old friend who worked, and still works, supervising production of a well-known deodorant. He used to play a lot of tennis, and now he does a lot of windsurfing. In Long Valley I smoked a lot of dope, and I covered the suburbs.

Those are unsettled towns, in-between places where people live who, by and large, work somewhere else and get transferred a lot. People in the suburbs do their best to keep in motion community enterprises such as the Little League, the planning commission, and the library, yet to me they seemed mostly to stay in motion themselves. The suburban station wagon is the Flying Dutchman of modern life. It glides in circles, among schools and playing fields and shopping malls.

I went off to Asia. After eight months on the road there I got a job in Kathmandu, teaching American English to Nepali university students for whom this language is the magical key that opens the world. I liked my students, though I never understood how they kept so clean. Kathmandu is a pretty dirty city, and in monsoon season I had to pedal my black Indian Hercules bicycle to school with a second set of clothes in a bag. What I was wearing would get wet mud up and down it in splatters and fans. Changed, I would squish into class (I only had one pair of shoes), and my poised, cherubic students would be waiting with copybooks open and legs primly crossed, crisp and shoe-shined and spotless.

"How do you do that?" I would implore.

"Do what, sir?" they would ask, and they would giggle at me, which they did often.

The Kathmandu Valley is a fertile, anciently settled tray set on the shoulders of high green hills, with the mountains behind. It has always been a crossroads of Asia, and its Hindus, native Buddhists, and Tibetan refugees observe interwoven ritual calendars through the cycle of each year. Other Western temporaries and I would watch, pressed to the edges of thronging crowds, as the ceremonies nudged each season into the next, from dust and heat to monsoon, to harvest, to the time of animal sacrifice, and to the new year lit by tiny lamps.

Among the colorful array of westerners in Kathmandu, many of course were pursuing oriental arts, knowledge, practices. To me this made them seem to be doing a kind of t'ai chi, some slow, patterned, alien dance. It was not our place and never genuinely our dance.

One afternoon in class my students and I, exploring English adjectives, came upon "exotic." I said, "Do you know, in America, people think that Kathmandu is exotic?" And my students, always polite but never sure if I knew what I was talking about, giggled and suggested that perhaps I meant to be funny about this—surely such a tradition-bound, isolated place, which they knew too well, could never be exotic.

"No," I said, "it's true."

"Sir," they said, "you can go anywhere in the world that you want, can you not?"

And I said, "yes, pretty much, that's true, too."

When I returned to America the streets were unnervingly clean, but I got used to that. Long Valley, New Jersey, had become a corporate suburb. There was no barnyard house full of oddballs any more. For a while I worked for Bionic Erectors, an outfit that put up, took down, and moved around modular office partitions. We Erectors wore black T-shirts and we'd swarm into corporate work-warrens to rearrange the tunnels and the cul-de-sacs, and as I worked, I wondered where I would go. If we don't have a place, we are inescapably, I think, looking for one. Arriving there finally—if we ever do—we may recognize our place, because it makes sense; and because, at least momentarily, we have dropped our guard.

The afternoon I came to Vermont I was hung over, as I say: There had been a night in bars in Hoboken, and my mouth had dried and my head throbbed. It hurt. On a bus in the afternoon I came into Montpelier, this capital that is a small town pressed between steep green hills. A friend who lives nearby had said he would meet me after work. So there was time to look around.

It was a late-spring day. The air was soft. I walked the streets, looking at the maple trees that shade these sidewalks and the porches of these well-tended, turn-of-the-century homes. The bookstore on Main Street was not a chain-store clone—it was a trove inside, dim and alluring and stacked high with volumes. A stuffed chair had been set in the corner for reading. Down the street a small, independent movie house in a storefront had a film showing from Australia, "Winter of Our Dreams." At the traffic light on the corner of State and Main the signal chirped like a bird, inviting me to come across.

It was coming into evening and it was a Friday; released people walked easily in the streets, socializing in the new, warm, after-winter time. The long late daylight sifted around them, darkness having retracted for the season. My friend apologized because, he said, there wasn't much to do in this little town. But I was wondrous and relaxed, the evening was alight, and I laughed.

Now it's a spring day again but it's raining, and there is massacre in the world. There is terror and terrible addiction and savagery among strangers, among the intimate; childhood is ripped up and stolen from children, it happens everywhere. People are bewildered and disconnected from what they see and hear. We feel this in Vermont, too, but not always so closely; the bad clamor of the general world is softened here because people are decent to each other. Sometimes I worry that a person who lives in a place like this one, which makes sense and is peaceable, is somehow abdicating. Maybe I should be down there in the lowlands getting crushed into commuter cars and polluted and angry or anesthetized and affluent with the other well-advantaged white people.

But, no. There are much better reasons to stay. It is not just that this is a good town, in a congenial and beautiful state. It is a fruitful environment. In their quiet way, places like Montpelier can be, and I think are, fulcrums for a better-changing world.

People try things that are possible here, in a place that is small and has room but that mingles with sophistication—that can make use of up-to-date communications and ideas and technologies yet has this starchy tradition of tolerance and liberty, of letting the odd and different be, of self-governance, of not disapproving as people try.

I look on as people I know have engineered a statewide effort that may give towns the means to deal with rapid development; have reinvented New England farming on small, chemical-free, market-attuned operations; have created gardening-to-learn projects in local schools; have pioneered a growing exchange of schoolchildren, then adults, between Vermont and the Soviet Union; have set up adventurous theater companies in a refitted country church, an old prefab barn, an Odd Fellows' Hall; have organized a community land trust that can make home ownership affordable again and keep it that way; have built a small college that works to give adults from difficult, disadvantaged, and abused backgrounds entry into professional careers.

It is possible to roam around Vermont and hear music, played by people who live here, that is, Jamaican, Appalachian, Ethiopian, American jazz, Chicago blues, Trinidad steel band, East European klezmer, Scandinavian string, European medieval, classical Indian, Indonesian gamelan, and God knows what else. In this place, what I mean is, there are gardeners everywhere, cultivating all sorts of living strains.

Me, I write feature stories for a big out-of-state newspaper. It's pretty good work, but it's not entirely mine and I am still restless. Not, any more, to go elsewhere; it's less clear to me what my unsettlement is. People do these venturesome things and I look on, fidgety, urgent somehow, still struggling to get in from the outside.

Outside just now, as I sit and think about this, it is raining on Main Street. This is late spring and it has rained and rained. You wonder when the season will change, though you know it is changing; yet all there seems to be is rain, maybe a warmer rain than it was a month or two months ago, but wet and dismal all the same.

When I first came up here I worked on a rural road cutting and shaping hardwoods for a cabinetmaker. Most of the neighbors on that road were down-country transplants, and what I noticed was that this seemed like a Third World for white people. There wasn't a lot of money. People helped each other, traded labor. Often livelihoods were pieced together of different pursuits. Much of the land was owned, and much of the economy controlled, from outside the state, by people who came here not at all or only for holidays.

Of course, Vermont is not some remote, bankrupted ex-colony. In a way it is the center of the world. This may be the place where a sustainable, productive, and decent postindustrial society has the best chance (if there is such a chance, if we still have one) of germinating—because Vermont is a rooted democracy in a sophisticated age, because it is a hard place and there is community, and because industrial ruination didn't happen here, the state was bypassed. For decades after the Civil War, Vermont's population was draining; now it is refilling, with relocated characters like me. Some truly seem harmonized. Their apple tree and their pickle crop are both symbols and reality, expressive to their hand; they dwell in their rural life and speak of it soon and easily. Others still are edgy and uncertain, not here that long and a little too restive yet to write to you as adopted scions of the New England earth. Yet here we also are.

I was in that cabinet shop so I could work part-time and write in the mornings. When the shop began to be successful, I left. My history in Vermont has been spotted ever since with what seems to be failure. Living here I wrote a book about traveling in Asia, which a large number of publishers have turned down. I wrote a story for children, to which the same thing has happened. I got married, and now I am getting divorced. I keep trying to start something in my old-fashioned copybook, or on a sturdy typewriter I picked from a pile at the end of a driveway, or at this portable computer that clacks here as the rain drips outside and cars swish through the water. I don't know what happens, where or why my internal circuit disconnects. I start new tries with genuine emotion; then things get turbulent and anguishing and I get very busy and in time what I started is lost, I'm on dry ground.

I have a boy now. He is most important of all. I want him absolutely to grow up in a world that makes sense, which is green and humanistic. When he is with me, we go out between rain spells and he jumps in every puddle, he works his feet to make the water pattern out and splash. He looks at me and laughs. He dances. He gets his sneakers wet to the socks. My boy is a natural.

But for me all this—this living, feeling for your place, trying to produce something good as you deal with breakups and failures and separation, this lasting from winter into spring—is painful. I think this is so for nearly everyone, everywhere. The thing is not to give up. To keep beginning, keep opening yourself to do what you can—to work and play and live from this same cracked and filling heart. In bumpy, long-wintered northern New England, what we are given is a grounded and still human-scale way of living and the chance to struggle. And where there is such struggle, isolating yet communal, eroding yet refilling, here—anywhere—is the shared, hopeful, anguishing center of the world.

My boy and I watched the water in the break-of-spring flood. Below the house where he lives, there is a one-lane bridge across a stream, and the boy was delighted at the roiling clamor down there. He ran from one side of the bridge to the other and back, and he looked down at the brown water as it surged and jumped among the rocks. The boy was newly conscious of the world: His face was open wide and he imitated this roaring sound, which the stream had broken into that day after a winter's locked silence. Then the boy did a dance, his dance, on the bridge. He hopped from one springy leg to the other—and when he stopped and plopped one foot in the mud and lifted it with a sucking sound, he and I watched the small footprint fill with water.

Some weeks after, we walked out in the still-drenching rain to look at the garden we had planted. We made the mutual error of stepping into it—now our shoes were hopelessly muddy, heavy with mud, we were a mess. While we stood there anyhow, the rain dripping off us, I looked for seedlings, too early to find them; and he looked at the mud.

This essay has been a dance around clichés, and I hope I have not stepped in them too much. I suppose what I mean the mud to stand for—what the proper Asian kids never got on them, what I am finally messing into, here in Vermont, what my boy dances in, fascinated, so easily—is not just being grounded physically in our lives but stepping into the morass that is our own personal, mostly internal world. This is what can come to mean something. It is easy just to move to a country place; you only have to figure out how to make a living, and you can do that. It's good for you to have to be inventive, to find what your capacities are. But that's just an adjustment to a different place; it doesn't answer the issue that just about everyone either faces or runs away from, in this day. How do we make something fruitful of ourselves, of our lives? How do we start to do the same for our world?

It isn't so plain any more, the answer to that. Even in a good, quieter, and still-green place like this one, the old structures of meaning and purpose and community and livelihood are eroding with the old life of isolation and the dairy-farm economy. It is up to us, the mix of us who live here now, to transform what remains of Vermont's way of life into something that preserves its small-scale decency yet is more connected to the wider world full of possibility. This struggle for rooted transformation in Vermont is almost never without conflict or rancor, but we can do it here, and we are trying.

Maybe my own struggle is more lastingly personal than many others', or maybe this is just the springtime rain I am getting through. Outside, Main Street is turning green—the maple trees have sprouted their summertime shade, the grasses are richly filling in. I think we must find our humanity, no matter how much of a mess this gets us in. Nothing we begin can broaden, bring real reward, or last if we are not, in the process, becoming ourselves.

What I see in Vermont is respect for that effort. I've come to believe that it's this becoming human—becoming grounded and connected again, becoming decent to each other and to the land, becoming actual productive people again—that is the heart of what this place has to offer American society. It's not scenery or unbuilt-upon property, not springtime Town Meeting or clap-boarded villages or a countrified way of life. What's happening here is more complex, and simpler. In a world of too many cold and corrosive realities, this is a warm place, after all. Vermont is a state of the possible.

On Main Street, It's Raining   27

Some Things We Do for Lamb

Don Mitchell

One cold, snowy night during "lambing season" of the year my son turned three, an unlikely sequence of events contrived to give his face a permanent scar. After far too many hours attending birth's wet miracle, I had trudged home from the barn in the wee hours and peeled off clothes made stiff from frozen amniotic fluids. I felt mightily discouraged: Trying to avoid catastrophic winter storms, I had scheduled our lamb crop to arrive at the end of March. Notwithstanding the calendar date, though, we were catching a stretch of weather more worthy of January than the first week of spring. Newborns in such circumstances, without round-the-clock attention, have a way of curling up and effortlessly dying.

All but fast asleep on my feet, I shambled toward the bedroom that lay one step down, in those days, from our adjoining kitchen; in the dark, stepping down, I landed with my full weight on the back of our aged German shepherd—Storm—who had arrayed his considerable bulk so as to sleep guarding the door. Storm raised his head and yelped, then relaxed when I apologized and stumbled off his furry spine.

Four paces away, the family cat—Guava—lay sleeping in the same bed as my wife and child. Hearing the startled bark of her nemesis, Guava sprang to life and snarled, swiping with one paw out into the middle distance. Then, apparently convinced it was a false alarm, she sheathed her hypodermic claws and settled back to sleep.

Several seconds later, my son let out a frightened scream. But then he, too, fell back into dreamland. All was quiet again.

Then, by moonlight, climbing into bed, I saw the stream of blood dripping down his mauled cheek and soaking the white pillowcase.

I shook awake my wife, Cheryl, and together we woke Ethan to explain that he had just been seriously injured. We phoned the hospital and described the wound to a doctor on call in the emergency room, then followed his advice and pulled the flaps of skin shut with two butterflies fashioned from adhesive tape. At a more rational, less exhausted time of year we doubtless would have rushed our baby into town for stitches, effecting a more cosmetic closure of the wound. One tends to lose a certain sense of proportion, though, three weeks into lambing. The relative weight of things gets easily confused. In the barn, dozens of life-and-death dramas keep unfolding around-the-clock, demanding all one's energies; after a while, real life can take a backseat. Even a fairly serious cat scratch can seem trivial or relatively unimportant.

I set the alarm to allow a couple hours' rest, then tumbled into bed with Ethan and my wife. There were several more ewes who appeared to be in labor, out there in the frigid barn. Half a dozen more lambs might be born before the dawn, and I wanted to greet them with the benefit of forty winks.

Nowadays — a decade later — any lambs born or not born on that night are long departed. And with time the long, thin scar on my son's cheek has grown familiar as a dimple. Only strangers seem to pay it conscious attention. Sometimes, though, the light will cross the planes of his face in such a way that one must notice; whenever that happens, I reproach myself for valuing the husbandry of sheep a bit too dearly that exhausted night, at the clear expense of other, vastly dearer charges.

Perhaps it shouldn't have to be so obsessive, this gentle business of husbanding sheep. Of shepherding. When Cheryl and I launched our flock in 1976, the goal was simply to create a grazing tool that could keep the weeds chewed down on the chunk of Vermont farmland that we had rashly purchased. We did not hope to make big bucks, but neither did we expect to lose our shirts. In any case, we felt that keeping livestock ought to give us a wide range of shared concerns with our Yankee neighbors, most of whom were prosperous dairy farmers; we hoped our daily lives would be enriched, as theirs seemed to be, by enforced attunement with the cycles of nature. Changing seasons—heat and cold, light and dark, drought and flooding. Times to reap and times to sow. To breed and bring forth young and rear them. What could be a more benign, uplifting source of rural pleasure than to manage a small flock in consonance with these steady undulations of New England's harsh and splendid climate?

What came as a surprise was the discovery that farmers do not so much work with nature as conspire against it—and that nature, in its implacable way, seems fully dedicated to conspiring right back. Summer follows winter quite predictably, of course, but from day to day the chances are good that capricious natural events will interfere with any flock's best interests. Too much rainfall or too little, and the sheep are bound to suffer. Too much grass or not enough, and their long-term prospects will be seriously jeopardized. Throw in predation, parasites, pneumonia, foot rot, mastitis, poisonous plants, and a score of other less-well-known catastrophes, and the sheer daily persistence of one's animals can, at times, seem to be an ongoing miracle. But it is a miracle for which shepherds come to fight, relying on whatever depths of strength and cunning they can muster.

The shepherds' cause has certainly been helped along, in recent years, by the advent of portable electric-fencing systems. This signal revolution has occurred in my career as shepherd, but surely my compatriots for four or five millenia have fantasized having just such a tool for the management of grazing stock. Rather than enclose, say, a thirty-acre pasture and turn my 100-ewe flock loose to roam it all summer long, I now "mob-stock" them on the merest two-acre paddocks—postage stamps, no more—and force the sheep to graze each tiny plot quite intensively before shuffling them along into the next enclosure. Such rotational-grazing systems tend to result in more forage tonnage and better forage quality, in the regular interruption of the life cycles of various debilitating stomach worms, and in relative safety from marauding canine predators, both wild and domestic. They also result in a fairly aerobic fence-moving chore, which requires a couple hours' labor every third day in a grazing season that can extend over seven months.

Those who play with fire can expect to get burned; those who commit themselves to fooling routinely with electric fence chargers can expect a fair number of shocking episodes, if only through the carelessness bred by the familiar. Chargers come in several different types, for different purposes. Some boast a relatively low-voltage shock but of fairly long duration, adequate to fry weeds to a crisp, should they dare to grow up and touch the hot wire; other chargers spit out an extremely short-duration pulse of whopping magnitude—5,000 volts for 3/10,000 of a second, say—so that the merest sting can make a grown man sit right down and cry. *This* grown man has, anyway.

All fence chargers, though—at least on the day they are sold—are so calibrated as to prevent a person from getting "hung up" on an electric fence. Initially, a muscle stimulated by electric shock may undergo a spasm of contraction; the human hand, laid across a hot fence, may involuntarily close tight around it when the pulse sizzles down the line. If there's not enough slack time in between pulses—that is, if the calibration isn't right—the hand might not fly off before the next shock comes along to force one's fingers to grip again. This is the condition known as getting hung up on a fence, and it is no laughing matter. Repeated shocking can have profound health consequences for both sheep and human beings, up to and including heart arrhythmia and death.

The pulse-and-duration characteristics of fence chargers are designed to obviate any risk of getting hung up on a fence. Fence chargers do get old, though, and can lose their calibration. Half a dozen years ago, I was simultaneously caring for my two-year-old daughter and moving our sheep from one electrically fenced paddock into another. Anais sat beneath a tree some distance from the newly erected fence line, learning about clover; I spoke to her as I worked, at length opening a temporary breach between one paddock and the next. To our mutual delight, the entire flock went bounding through the gap to where the grass was clearly greener. But Ginger—the 115-pound Great Pyrenees guard dog who had replaced old Storm, and who lived on the pasture to keep coyotes from our sheep—had a somewhat different thought. She ducked behind me, danced into the clear, and started loping toward the far horizon, bent on seeing more of the world than the next two-acre rotational-grazing paddock. I closed the fence and turned it on, then set off to catch the dog and lead her back to reshoulder her immense responsibilities.

The dog did not go far, in fact, no farther than some fifty yards. She chased a startled woodchuck into its burrow and then knelt before the hole, white tail curled above her back and flying in the breeze. I had just grabbed Ginger's collar—scolding her, but amiably—when I turned to see Anais tottering over toward the fence. I shouted, but my daughter stuck firmly to her agenda: She reached out and grabbed a wire. Then, with a sickening feeling I won't easily forget, I saw her little body twitch as though she were a marionette jerked by some cruel string. After the pulse had passed, her hand did not come off. She screamed once, and then she stopped screaming.

I let go the dog and ran; when I reached Anais, she was plainly falling into shock. I scooped her up, but her hand was fastened to that wire and the next pulse rippling down the fence zapped us both together. Coming to my senses, I dove at the fence charger and tore its cables from the battery terminals that kept it fed with juice. Anais's tiny hand relaxed, and she sat down in a stunned daze.

I lifted her into my arms and started running toward the house; Ginger might stray all the way to New Hampshire, but this time I intended to keep my priorities straight. On the way, my daughter's respiration and pulse and color gradually returned to normal. Then she started crying, a sure sign of recovery. I explained about the fence; she nodded in apparent comprehension. By the time we reached the house, I knew there was no need to fear. She had had a shock—or ten—but there was no lasting damage. Luck, I guess, and rubber-soled sneakers, which afforded her a measure of insulation from the ground each pulse was seeking.

I replaced the fence charger. I learned it was safer to do fencing chores while she was napping—even if she woke up in the house to find herself alone.

I don't think of myself as a reckless individual, nor—looking back on nearly fifteen years of shepherding—do I seem to be unusually accident-prone. It is a fact of family farming, though, that the details of everyday life share an awkward, jagged boundary with those of a physically demanding, inherently dangerous occupation. One can exercise greater or lesser caution, trying to create a place where lambs and children both may thrive; what one cannot do, though, is eradicate the very possibility of harm.

Harm came to me, some years back, in an episode of attentive sheep husbandry that still gives me nightmares, along with chronic sinus discomfort. All my sheep came down with keds— a small, brown, blood-sucking external parasite—and I set out to treat them with a state-of-the-art drug of marvelous toxicity. Spotton was its brand name, and the fine print on the plastic bottle read:

Fenthion (0,0-Dimethyl-0-4-methylthio-mtolyl phosphorothioate) in 20% solution.

I cracked the bottle open and caught a whiff of warmed-over chemical death. The accompanying brochure made lively reading. So toxic was this wonder drug, one had only to part the wool on an adult sheep's back and pour two ccs of Spotton onto the skin, and it would soak down into the animal and render its blood toxic to all blood-sucking external parasites for a period of several days. Careless overdosing, needless to say, could render the animal's blood quite toxic to the animal itself...an ultimate but costly cure for keds. As for the person administering Spotton to a herd or flock, the brochure cautioned that he or she ought to wear sturdy rubber gloves and avoid spilling a drop. It wouldn't take a lot of Spotton, soaked into a human's skin, to produce symptoms startlingly analogous to those caused by muscular dystrophy.

A low-tech way to treat each individual in a flock of sheep is to herd them in the barn and build, adjacent to the door, a working pen out of half a dozen wooden hurdles. Small groups of sheep can then be crowded into the working pen, where they defeat each other's efforts to escape the shepherd's ministrations.

Some Things We Do for Lamb   **33**

As each sheep is treated with the medication of the day, the shepherd marks its nose with colored chalk; this serves to prove that each sheep has been handled once, without any double dosing. After a subgroup of eight to ten sheep in the working pen receives its treatment, those animals can be released to go back out on pasture.

I had used the working-pen technique to trim ewes' feet, to give them wormers, to offer them shots against tetanus and abortive illness. There was no reason why it shouldn't work for administering Spotton, too—and it did work for administering Spotton, except that when the last group of animals had been released, I found one adolescent, high-strung ewe who would not pay a visit to the doctor. She hid in a corner of the barn, playing invisible; I chased her to the working pen and trapped her there, all by herself.

Sheep, it must be pointed out, just hate to be all by themselves. Picking up the Spotton bottle, I moved toward her gingerly. In a state of panic, she sprang forward and up, butting her thick head directly at my nose; the last thing I heard was a sharp, ear-splitting crack!—just as though a pistol had been fired at close range. I fell over backwards in excruciating pain and promptly passed unconscious.

When I came to, the jumpy ewe had vaulted the hurdles of the working pen and found her freedom. Letting one sheep go untreated obviated, I well knew, the entire ked-eradication drill; it was just a matter of time before she managed to reinfect the others. But that was the least of my problems. Blood streamed out of both my nostrils, and my nose appeared to have been quite professionally broken. When I sat up, swooning, I looked down to see the Spotton bottle spilling lethal Fenthion into the bedstraw a scant few inches from my leg.

I rolled away fast and staggered home; minutes later, Cheryl had me lying in our car's backseat while she sped me to the hospital.

My nose proved quite repairable, though since that day it hasn't worked as well as I recall it once did. I seem unusually prone to congestion and sniffles and sinus headaches—tolerable burdens, but burdens nonetheless. The real test of nerve, though, was to get through the first several days after the accident wondering if and when I would start displaying symptoms of muscular dystrophy. And would I know? And would my dear ones—wife, son, daughter—have the heart to tell me? Had I irrevocably altered my life by an unlucky episode with fancy insecticide?

Apparently not—although it's possible, I suppose, that everyone I know has been conspiring to humor me these past several years. The thing is, I feel like I came that close. But so, in countless other ways, do all who live and work on farms: men and women, grandpas, grandmas, adolescents, little children. On the face of things, it would be hard to conceive a more pacific occupation than husbanding a flock of sheep; the fact is, everybody in my family now bears scars won in this bucolic labor. And yet, shepherding has become intertwined with what I can only call the meaning of our lives, here. There are always difficulties. There are certain risks and will be. But we don't regret contriving to make these green fields say Baaa! Each of us has come to love the things we have to do for lamb.

The Gentrification of Vermont

Norman Runnion

I've always had a theory about such luxury holes as Stratton and Sugarbush. The skiers or the golfers or the condominium owners who populate these resorts in whatever high season occurs during the year do not, in my imagination, drive to them. They don't come by plane, bus, or boat, either. They're all transported ethereally, as if they were on a flying carpet express (air-conditioned and enclosed, of course) between their first homes and their second or third domicile at Stratton or Sugarbush.

David Chase, a Vermont humorist and writer who lives in Brattleboro, once said he liked Stratton (he should know; as a carpenter, he helped build a lot of that stuff) but he never was under any illusion that he was actually in Vermont when he went there.

My worry, which has gained great strength in recent years, is that Vermont is becoming Strattonized—or gentrified—to an extent no one believed possible even just a few years ago in the mid-1980s.

In the early 1970s, the Vermont legislature enacted Act 250 to try to control subdivision development, which in those days of "The Beckoning Country" was beckoning too many of the wrong kind of people: developers who wanted to make a quick profit at the expense of both the environment and the public. The legislature set up a process whereby any subdivision development would have to meet ten land-use criteria to be acceptable. Those rules put a quick halt to a lot of shabby practices, such as trying to place a development on ledge where the sewerage runoff headed straight into the nearest drinking water source.

Act 250 has been hailed as one of the pioneering state environmental laws in the United States. But the law has had no impact on the gentrification of Vermont twenty to twenty-five years later—absolutely none. Actually, Act 250 probably has assisted gentrification with a reverse twist: By trying to ensure vacation home development of some responsibility, it has helped Vermont retain its image of environmental quality. Vermont is a state of mind to most people—even to those of us who live here—and it is that state of mind, or "quality of life," as the travel brochures might have it, that makes Vermont more attractive than, say, northern New Jersey as the site for a vacation home.

A couple of images of Stattonization stand out. Many years ago, I was covering a very hot session of the Vermont legislature involving a high degree of political partisanship. At the end of a day in which emotions on all sides in all corners of the statehouse were intense and even bitter, one of the key participants and I went to dinner at a restaurant at the Sugarbush resort in Warren, some thirty miles from Montpelier. The idea was to escape the Vermont political hothouse of Montpelier, and we sure did that. In fact, we escaped "Vermont." Our dining companions in that restaurant were visitors—not to the real Vermont but to the upscale, Sunday *New York Times Magazine* concept of Vermont. This is a four-color panorama of ski slopes, condominiums, and nice people who, if they weren't in Sugarbush, might be photographed lolling on the sun deck of a cruise liner. The conversation we overheard at adjoining tables concerned the vacation home they were going to buy, or the nice little restaurant the other side of Warren, or the friends who were coming up from New York this weekend. But Vermont was an abstraction to them, sort of Fire Island North.

That was when I first had this ghostly feeling: These people didn't drive to Warren. They just *arrived* there from, as David Chase puts it, Someplace Else.

The same feeling occurred a couple of years ago when I was invited to play golf at Stratton, which to a golfer is a delight because it's a wonderful course, as befitting a world-class resort.

People from Someplace Else were all over the course, in designer golf clothes. The young men and women, tanned and healthy, looked as though they had just magic-carpeted into Stratton from a surfing outing in Newport Beach, California. At lunch in the Stratton clubhouse, an acquaintance of my host stopped by for a chat about his golf game. Later in the day, a couple of us went for a drive up one of Stratton's mountain paths to a development where most of the houses cost in excess of $1 million. Wow! They're on a quarter of an acre with a superb, panoramic view of their neighbor's million-dollar house on another quarter acre. Anyhow, this guy, the one who talked about his golf game at lunch, lives in one of these palaces. "What does he do?" I asked. "He's one of the world's leading importers of casings." "Casings?" "Yeah, casings; you know, for sausages."

Here is a man who makes a business career out of intestines, and he's living in one hell of a nice house in Stratton when he's up for the weekend or summer, and I appreciate that. I don't envy him his money—he does his thing with intestines and I do mine writing—and I certainly think he has as much right to be in Stratton and playing golf as I do to live in Brattleboro and play golf on the same Stratton course as he does when someone else will pay my greens fee. There is as much a place for intestine importers in Vermont as there is for dairy farmers. But the dairy farmers are dying. The other guys are not.

This process is accelerating. Southern Vermont, when I first came to it in the early 1960s, was truly rural, in person and in deed. I, on the other hand, was truly city, seeking a change, which is the same excuse for most of us who have moved here from Someplace Else. In my own case, Someplace Else was the likes of Chicago, New York, Paris, London, and Washington, D.C., where in the course of fifteen years I had lived the usual chaotic life of a journalist. For most of the last quarter century I've still lived the usual chaotic life of a journalist, except that it's been in a small Vermont town, and that was a choice that transcended everything.

I'm anything but unique in that choice, but the paradise of my choosing—Vermont—is hardly the same place today. The landscape is changing, the life-styles are altering, and, most sad of all, the old Vermonters are dying off. They had replaced their fathers, their grandfathers, and their great-grandfathers, but no one is replacing *them* today.

In 1966 I bought a house in Dummerston, just to the north of Brattleboro, and, following the fashion of the day for many people who lived near Dummerston Center on the top of the hill, I called on Mert Hazelton to plow my driveway in the winter. Merton Hazelton plowed everyone's driveway in Dummerston Center in those days. He was the prototypical Vermont farmer. The Hazelton orchards—run by himself and his son, Donald—raised apples and strawberries, and their sugarhouse, across the road from the proto-typical Congregational church, which itself was across the road from the prototypical Grange Hall, was prototypical.

Mert Hazelton was not a man to waste words. If he had ever sat down to dinner with Calvin Coolidge, Mert would have thought to himself afterwards, "That man talks too much." When I asked Mert to plow my drive that winter, he just looked at me, sizing me up. Then he gave me one of his apples. No words were exchanged. He gave me the apple and I ate it, right there, consummating the contract. When the first snow fell, there was Mert Hazelton on his tractor. His bills for this chore were astonishing. Vermont had a lot of snowstorms that year, and Mert's charges varied with the storm. Some would be for $2.40; others for $3.10; a nor'easter might bring a charge of $4.25. I once figured that he had some obscure, Mert-only formula of charging by the inch of snow that fell. A year later, after a season that cost me something like $36.00 for snow removal, Mert dropped by the house and said he wouldn't be plowing next year, he was getting on. I bought a snowblower. It cost me $350.00—about ten years' worth of Mert Hazelton.

When Mert Hazelton died in the winter of 1980, I said about him in *The Reformer*, "He was all that we value in Vermont. He was hard-working, a man of the soil, a man of community—and a remarkably devoted and tight-knit community Dummerston Center is. He was a town officer, he served his church, and his grange. Fortunately, Donald Hazelton carries on these great tradi-tions. And they are so necessary. Vermont is modernizing so quickly that traditions are in danger of being forgotten. Merton Hazelton's deeply rooted ties to Vermont's past always reminded us of this state's true values—values that we want to retain."

Well, that sounds nice. But nine years later, Donald Hazelton packed it in. Modern Vermont had become too much for him.

When Donald Hazelton was fifty-nine, in 1989, he sold the fifteen acres of orchards that had been his whole life and that of his father. It was a combination of factors that hurt him, including The Great Alar Scare, in which actress Meryl Streep proclaimed throughout the nation and the world that one bite of an Alar-sprayed apple would lead not only to deprivations of the human condition but might create psychic disturbances preventing young people from attending her movies. Many Vermont farmers were appalled at the loss of Alar, which they considered far less dangerous than driving through traffic to get to a supermarket. Alar was a chemical that kept the apples on the trees longer, enabling more of them to get to market. "Alar was my warehouse," Don Hazelton said. But in health-conscious America, Streep had the upper hand, to the Hazeltons' shock.

As Bunny Hazelton, Don's wife, put it, "What farmer is going to put stuff on his apples that would hurt his children and his grandchildren? But no. You get movie stars and 'experts' who get the whole country in such a doggone scare that the kids are scared to eat apples. People want perfect fruit, but they don't want to pay for it. They don't realize what goes into it, the costs, the labor, the tractor repair, year-round pruning and spraying for insects."

But Alar is off the market, and it took Donald Hazelton's way of life with it. That, and the natural disasters that accompany the life of any farmer: hail that damaged the strawberry crop, an ailment—either insects or acid rain—that is wiping out the sugar maples, and endless streams of paperwork. He's through as a farmer, and he's looking for a job in the other world, the world of factories, shops, and condominiums.

The orchards themselves still produce the McIntoshes and Macouns for which the Hazeltons were famous. The fifteen acres of trees were bought by a Dummerston neighbor, Dwight Miller, whose orchards are as well known as the Hazeltons', and whose Vermont roots are so deep that they go back to the original settlers of Dummerston. Dwight Miller is getting tired of the fight, too. But unlike Don Hazelton, Miller still wants to carry on.

If a Vermont accent had been invented, Dwight Miller would own the patent. Just listening to him talk is worth the trip. But what he says these days is not the voice of an optimist: "With agriculture in this state, you never made any money, but you enjoyed the work. Now, we're still not making any money, and the fun's gone right out of it."

Vermont is reaching the point where it may have more condominiums than cows. That means, in Dwight Miller's opinion, that it's time for a choice. Vermonters, he says, must decide whether they want to continue replacing cows with more condominiums. Some already have made that choice. That's why Stratton exists, and it's why Sugarbush exists, and it's why a lot of "prime agriculture soil" is headed for development. If a farm is picturesque enough for a *Vermont Life* photograph, it's a great spot for a condo.

The trend toward change in Vermont accelerated in the early 1980s to the point where it's irreversible. The enormous middle-class migration to Vermont is in large part responsible. Technology came to Burlington in the form of International Business Machines, and the astonishing—in size—IBM complex in Essex Junction has produced a life-form and life-style of its own, all of it white-collar and well paid. Equally, the arrival of the interstate in the 1960s changed southern Vermont forever, coinciding as it did with the explosion in popularity of skiing as a sport.

In the late 1960s, when we were finished around midnight on Fridays producing the Saturday morning *Reformer*, we would adjourn to the Latchis Hotel bar on lower Main Street for a midnight beer. The Latchis Hotel and cinema was an art deco masterpiece when it was built in Brattleboro in the 1930s, but by the late 1960s it basically was a dump, bypassed and forsaken by motels on the outskirts, a fate befitting most central-core hotels in modern times. Yet it was cheap, it was clean, and it was a place to stay, and a lot of skiers would camp there Friday night after the drive from New York City to ready for a day's skiing at Mount Snow or Stratton the next day. Stratton in particular didn't have much in the way of amenities in those days. At any rate, those Friday nights were convivial and a lot of fun, and there was a lot of companionship in the bar late at night among those of us who worked in Brattleboro and the crowd up from New York for the weekend.

Twenty years later, the skiers have become people from Some-place Else, and when they aren't whizzing through Brattleboro en route to motel paradise in Winhall or Dover, they are passing ethereally overhead, transported through time and space from Park Avenue to their condos. In the 1960s, most skiers came for the fun of it, to slide down the hill on snow, all to be done without spending a great deal of money, which is what attracted them to the Latchis. Now, those same ski slopes are called "destination resorts," and they're filled with vacation homes and fine hotels and excellent restaurants, all of which can be paid for with credit cards.

Brattleboro's downtown, meanwhile, suffered the usual prob-lems generated by the presence of old hotels, lousy parking, and the growth of stores in the outskirts. Like many Main Streets, how-ever, it is now making a comeback. As some Americans rediscover their parents' love affair with "downtown," old stores have turned into fancy boutiques, restaurants sprout "continental menus," and the Latchis Hotel itself has been renovated to the point of gentrifi-cation. Thanks to the young descendants of the original owners, it is blossoming in beauty rather than withering in despair. This kind of gentrification, however, is good for Vermont, not because it is imposing new values on the state but because it is restoring much needed reminders of the past. Elizabeth Vineyard, vice president of the Latchis Hotel Corporation, said in the summer of 1989, following the grand opening of the remodeled building, "The Latchis is not just someone's private business, it's an integral part of the town's heritage and collective memory."

The new complex, with its refined rooms and modern the-aters, is, Vineyard said, a rare commodity "in a world of multiplexes floating in a sea of asphalt." Anyone who can coin a phrase like that can renovate an old hotel.

This is local-control gentrification, if you will, and is authentic, as against a proposal in the mid-1970s to dress up Brattleboro's Main Street by covering the town's individual architecture with white false fronts designed to create an image of Woodstock-South. That idea went nowhere. Jimmy Breslin, New York's latest incar-nation of Damon Runyan's Guys, once growled at me over the telephone, "Yeah, Brattleboro, I was there once. Lotsa red bricks." The red bricks remain red, and Woodstock remains white.

But there's an imposed gentrification that is encroaching on Vermont, and it is best symbolized by the concern of some agri-businessmen for the image of a cow. Brattleboro is the home of the Holstein Association, which employs a couple of hundred people in town whose awesome job it is to keep tabs on every Holstein cow in the world. The Holstein Association's computers track Holstein granddads, grandmas, uncles, aunts, and thousands of pounds of milk per udder, and all this information is used by dairymen and breeders throughout the world to both improve the breed and increase milk tonnage. Holstein's headquarters are in a wonderful old building not far from the Latchis Theater, and it is covered with ivy and has the solid look of an institution whose information about Holstein cows can be thoroughly trusted. A lot of agriculture experts visit Brattleboro to discuss those cows.

In 1988 Holstein's board of directors tried to offer the town of Brattleboro a non-negotiable deal: If you don't do what we want, they said, we'll move our headquarters to some other state and take our payroll with us.

As demands, the Holstein directors wanted to take over the Brattleboro Museum & Art Center, painstakenly converted by history lovers and art buffs from a decaying railroad station into one of the finest small museums in the country, and turn it into a museum about Holstein cows. The directors demanded that town officials make arrangements for the privately run museum to be given to them. Furthermore, Holstein's directors also demanded that the town and the state of Vermont combine to clean up—literally gentrify—the streets around the Holstein Association building.

Well, the plan blew up in Holstein's face. Townspeople were furious at being blackmailed, and the issue lay down to rest. But like a lot of things in Vermont, the confrontation started people thinking.

A private land trust bought a couple of old buildings in the South Main Street-Canal Street area and began to renovate them. A local builder purchased one of the biggest of the tenement buildings and said he would turn it into affordable housing. The selectmen enthusiastically backed both projects.

If all this does produce that most elusive of modern dreams, "affordable housing," then ordinary people will benefit. Unfortunately, history is against that kind of thing. In most such examples,

The Gentrification of Vermont   **43**

as gentrification occurs, rents and prices go up, the poor find it expensive (or "unaffordable," to use the modern code word) to live there, and the middle class moves in. This happened on Capitol Hill in Washington, D.C., and it could happen in Brattleboro, and it already is happening in other parts of Vermont around the ski resorts. And if we don't watch out, the only Holstein to appear in Vermont will be on a computer and not in a dairy farmer's pasture.

Then again, the newly gentrified Vermonters will need a couple of poor people around, not only as token Vermonters but because the poor don't expect much pay in return for their labors. Take the ultragentrified town of Grafton, for example, which has been restored, à la Williamsburg, Virginia, by the mega-rich Windham Foundation. Grafton is in the northern edge of Windham County, and it is full of beautiful homes and at times Beautiful People, and not long ago there was a proposal to put a trailer park on the outskirts. A trailer park in Grafton is like putting neon lights all over Mount Vernon saying, "George Washington slept here."

A Grafton resident called one of the executives of the Windham Foundation and demanded that he "do something" to stop that trailer park from coming to town. A couple of days later, she called again and said, "I've changed my mind. I think we could use those trailers." Asked a puzzled why, she replied, "Domestic help, particularly maids, is very hard to get, and those trailers probably would be a good source of domestic help."

When I related that tale not long ago to Thomas Salmon, who was governor of Vermont in the mid-1970s and also one of the best governors in the state's modern history, he was swept by shock. Salmon, like a lot of us—including all recent governors except Deane Davis—is from Someplace Else, yet his tenure as governor was marked by highly visible and often successful efforts to retain Vermont's soul. In particular, his brainchild was the Property Tax Relief Fund, whereby state money has been used to help a lot of poor and elderly Vermonters stay in their homes by assisting in the payment of their ever-soaring property taxes. This is the crux of Vermont's modern problems: Vermont is becoming too expensive for ordinary Vermonters who, caught in the encroaching tidal wave of money pouring into this state, are the ultimate victims of gentrification and Strattonization.

It is a tidal wave, too, sweeping up the Connecticut River valley along the trough provided by I-91. Between Northampton and Greenfield, Massachusetts, for example, the land used to be largely devoted to farms. But now factories and industries are springing up alongside the interstate, giving it the ominous beginning look of the New Jersey Turnpike. And Greenfield, the northern terminus of this expansion, is only ten miles south of the Vermont border.

The changes can't be stopped. The question of the era is, can they be directed?

People from Someplace Else always have moved to Vermont, beginning with the white settlers who established Fort Dummer on the banks of the Connecticut River, just south of Brattleboro, in 1724, thereby gentrifying land that until then had been exclusively the forest home of Indians. As Franklin D. Roosevelt said when he shocked the Daughters of the American Revolution in the 1930s, we're all immigrants. But these immigrants in New England, and their sons and daughters, created what has become the unique Vermont character, the very nature of a people whose independence of mind and spirit are stamped on the rocky soil of this hill country.

Vermont did not evolve politically, morally, or socially over the years to become an upper-class enclave for the pleasure seeker who at the same time wants to hire a maid living in some out-of-sight trailer park. If Vermont is to resist this encroachment, if it is to try to direct or divert or alter the current of change blowing in from points south, then it can only do so by having its citizens, new and old, reaffirm their allegiance to that which brought them here in the first place—Vermont.

This means getting involved.

Stephan Morse, a son of Newfane, pondered what he saw as the winds of change from his vantage point as executive director of the Windham Foundation. Newfane is one of southern Vermont's top tourist attractions for three essential reasons: the Windham County Courthouse, which graces the Newfane common as if reproduced live, and in living color, from the pages of Currier and Ives, and two superlative inns. But the real Newfane was hidden from those enjoying coq au vin in the eateries; it was a working people's town. But it has changed. Nowadays, Morse says, people live in Newfane, work in Brattleboro, shop in Keene, New Hampshire, and when they come back home, they don't talk with their neighbors and they don't go to Town Meeting.

I was fascinated a year or so ago by a trip to the Northeast Kingdom, and when I drove through Lyndonville, north of St. Johnsbury, there was a village parade in progress, and it was a lot of fun, and it slowed down the traffic, and you could look around Lyndonville and see that this was a Vermont town in the Vermont tradition. People lived there, worked there, shopped there, and attended Town Meeting. Newfane used to be like that. There isn't a Lyndonville to be found in all of Windham County, and one day there may not be a Lyndonville found in Lyndonville.

When I say that a path to Vermont's salvation means "getting involved," I mean it this way: People should live in Newfane, work in Brattleboro, shop in Keene, but when they get home, they damn well better go to Town Meeting.

Town Meeting's most frightening aspect is that it has become quaint, a media event. The *New York Times* sends a reporter to Town Meeting to write about how quaint local democracy is; and CBS sends a camera crew, and they photograph someone with a beard and pontificate how quaint Town Meeting is. But it's not quaint and it won't work and it isn't that ultimate cliché, "democracy in action," if no one cares what happens there.

Sure, most small-town Town Meetings still are well attended, because they're neighborly, because it's a good time for gossip, and because some minor decisions can be made. It is in the large towns where local control is vanishing, partly because of a sense of frustration on the part of citizens who realize they no longer have any real say over school and town budgets; and partly, if not mostly, because so many people have been caught up in the rat race. It was fashionable in the 1970s to say that people were fleeing the rat race to move to Vermont, but the race came with them.

The rat—i.e., the money chase, the ambition game, the keeping-up appearances—simply deserted the sinking urban ship and climbed aboard the maple leaf-strewn deck of Vermont. Getting involved requires a lot of energy, and if you're tired after a hard day's earning a dollar—or, in the case of many Vermont couples, a hard day on the part of both of them trying to earn enough cash in two jobs to not only finance a car but to pay property taxes—then it's difficult to summon up the energy to partake in "democracy." That's one reason the big money changes affecting Vermont—including but not limited to gentrification—have taken such a toll on this state's soul. It costs too much, and it takes too much time, to be a Vermonter.

There is a narrow way out. Citizens—new, old, and indifferent—need to get involved in their own government. On boards of selectmen and planning commissions and zoning boards, they can help determine the future of their town by trying to attract business and industry whose pay scales for working Vermonters are far beyond the small wages of the pleasure industry. Vermonters can afford to stay in Vermont if they're paid enough to live relatively well. Historically, this simply has not been the case.

This, of course, means that there must be that inevitable "balance" between the economy and the environment. But that balance is neither hard to define nor to find if Vermonters, with Vermont's interest at their very heart, get involved as selectmen and planners and zoners. The great danger to Vermont is that politically, power will be seized at the local level by the gentrifiers, the Last-Man-Iners, the Drawbridgers, the Not-In-My-Backyarders, who, having found gentrification a delight to their taste buds, want everyone to bask in picture windows that don't overlook trailers, tenements, or tramps.

The gentrifiers—defined once as "well born, not necessarily noble"—are grabbing hold of their version of Vermont. We need a new breed of gentrifiers—the truly noble—who, alongside Vermont's working people, want to grab it back.

Foliage Season

Andy Potok

Some say art is dead, others that it is long. Some are in it for the money, some for salvation. In a lulled, complacent society like ours, art's role might be to shock, awaken; in another, to record, to reflect on life or on itself. What interests me is that, no matter what the circumstances, art is difficult, not just in the making but in the understanding, that its creation requires great friction, its comprehension comes with great resistance. It is marvelous because of its complexity. The more you struggle the more you get.

Not everyone in the world agrees with this. Take my children for example. Their satisfaction with their kind of music mystifies me. My children are bright, they make informed decisions in the world. But if you asked me, I'd say that their music comes to them without benefit of interference and it goes straight to the reptilian part of the brain. I would say that their music is not art, it's entertainment. If it's easy, it's entertainment; if it's hard, it's art.

Then there's the matter of where you live. Place impinges on the art that's being made. There are places in the world that seem to be ripe for art, which, for better or worse, demand and inspire art's vital necessity, its urgency.

Take Vermont. A lot of us sit here, creating our art. It is a good quiet place in which to reflect, to gather one's world experience, but can these lovely hills and meadows unleash art that is a matter of life or death?

The sweet dream about this place is what makes people buy things that plainly say "Vermont" on the package, even if it's made

48

in New Jersey. That Vermont—vaguely clean, simple, and pure—is as insipid as nostalgia. It's an entertainment. It's Town Meeting with a chorus in overalls voting for what is good and true as the Trapp family hums tunes of democracy.

Now, take another Vermont attraction. Take foliage season. It too is frictionless, resistance free, like sunsets and sitcoms. I have always had problems with it, even before I lost my eyesight. Years ago, when I was still a painter and first bought my cozy farmhouse at the top of a hill, I reported the transaction to a sculptor friend who lived in the city and spent summers in an ugly rented bungalow on Long Island. In the glow of new ownership, I told him that I could look out my living room windows and see the Worcester range.

"Terrific," he said without enthusiasm.

Not thinking, I said that in autumn, the spread of color in those mountains before me was majestic.

He winced. "You can see that crap in the fall collection at Bloomingdale's," he said.

He had a point. As a matter of fact, I hate foliage season. Even when I could see, I was immune to the sheer obviousness of those E-Z listening combinations, God's own Muzak.

I think that my wife and my friends feel particularly sorry for my no longer being able to see foliage season. Well, let me tell you, it's the least of my problems.

"Why don't you write about foliage season?" my wife suggested. "You know, Andy, from your unique point of view. Write what you hear, what you smell, what it feels like."

Now, as I walk down my hill, clutching the harness of my wonderful Seeing Eye dog, Dash, I can indeed smell foliage season, the mild rot of dying leaves, the astringent plumes of wood smoke, pleasanter than diesel fuel but toxic nevertheless.

"Curmudgeon, crank," my friends yell out of the windows of their cars as they pass me walking on my dirt road that rustles with fallen leaves.

As Dash and I enter our quaint little village, his tail is wagging because we are in the middle of a crowd, a rare occurrence where we live. "It must be foliage season," I confide to my beautiful beast. The leaf peepers have gathered at the Methodist church. Their

Foliage Season   **49**

oversized cars are strewn throughout the village. And slowly, the pious folk wend their way to celebrate yellow, orange, and brown. For reasons aesthetic as well as spiritual, their revelry is as closed to me as the Wannssee Conference.

You don't paint foliage season, you paint in spite of it. You look for your inspiration elsewhere, for here in Vermont you are largely unencumbered by the insanity of the world. Even though a writer's passion must ripen in front of a blank piece of paper, the artist's before a white canvas, there are days when I crave the fire of out there, the life and passion of throngs, the urgency, gravity, the sheer weight of cities, nations, whole continents consumed by struggle.

My dilemma is increased by blindness that, in spite of the sanguine protestations of some, does impose limitations on what is possible. Even though my past history is thrill packed, Vermont plus blindness equals serious sensory deprivation.

I had arrived in America some six months after the outbreak of the Second World War, squeezed out of Poland by German tanks rolling in from the west, Russian ones from the east. We slipped into Lithuania as the border was closing, we crossed the ocean on the last boat out of Norway. As an adult many years later, I went back to Europe to live. When my first wife and I separated in Greece twenty-five years ago, I came to Vermont. I had had enough travel, enough movement and displacement. I wanted the stability of seeing my children board a yellow school bus every morning, of being a part of a community at rest. Vermont was a haven. The very name of the village where we settled was important. Plainfield. So simple, so American. Houses were available in towns with lively, resonant names like Adamant and Calais and Montpelier, but Plainfield suited me perfectly.

"Sometimes I feel I've been hiding out too long," I had recently told an old friend who remained in New York, where I grew up.

"Hiding?" she said, "I thought they'd put you in the Federal Witness Protection Program."

When Dash and I walk down my dirt road on the way to my office, I sometimes think that there are more dogs in sleepy Plainfield than at the start of the Alaska Iditarod. Every kind of runty cur, swaybacked hound, and flea-infested mongrel is yapping, baying, or snarling as we walk by. On the two-mile trek we pass Chelsea and Sadie, wave to Harley and Lila, try to sneak by the awful twin dachshunds who live in a log cabin. Some strain at their chains, yank at their ropes. Some run out to greet us, some follow us part of the way. In the village itself, the houses are alive with the sound of growling. We run the gauntlet, Dash and I, our hearts pounding.

This then is the nature of our early morning excitement. Aside from the relative silence of the country, these mutts structure my mind into a writing mode. They prepare me for my daily battle with words.

Often I long for something else. Last year I went back to Poland. It was not my first trip back as I have a serious love-hate relationship with the place. For instance: I consider myself an American, originally Polish. When I go back to Poland, I feel proud that I can still speak the language, that I have significant, formative memories there. But the Poles think otherwise. To them I am Jewish, not Polish. And I never feel more Jewish than when I go back to Poland. More Jewish is hardly the word for it. I feel like a Hassid at a DAR convention.

And here, at the widening of the Vistula, are my roots. I want to finally stand on a spot where others with my name have lived, been slaughtered, and are buried, where, like my neighbors in Vermont, I can trace back my ancestors a few hundred years. But more than that, standing on this perennial battlefield, I want clues as to why I am the way I am: a sap for romance, a brooder, a pessimist, a cynic, a crank. I want to know why my heart resonates to Andrzej Wajda films, to Tadeusz Konwicki novels, Zbigniew Herbert poems, why Polish humor and Polish stories satisfy my need to laugh and to cry.

A man comes into the patent office, tells the clerk he wants to register an invention, a new, more efficient mousetrap. From his bag he takes a small flat board with an exposed razor blade sticking out of its center. He reaches into his bag again, pulls out some ham, which he puts on one side of the blade, and then some cheese, which he puts on the other.

"The mouse will come up," the guy explains, "look to one side, see the ham, look to the other, see the cheese—ham? cheese? ham?

cheese? He won't be able to make up his mind and in the process he'll slit his own throat."

The clerk shrugs—he's seen it all—enters the patent in his books, gives the guy his receipt.

A week later, the man's back. He wants to register a new invention: an even more efficient mousetrap. He reaches into his bag, carefully extracts a small flat board with an exposed razor protruding from its center.

"Wait a second," says the patent officer, "you've already registered the same invention last week."

"This one's different," says the guy. He lays it out on the table and smiles. "That's it," he says. "Nothing else. Mouse will come up to the blade, turn to his right, 'What, no ham?' turn to his left, 'What, no cheese?' No ham? no cheese? no ham? no cheese...?' "

I am drawn to Poland like my dog is to the lamppost. While in harness and working, Dash knows that if he sniffs I will correct him, but he risks it for a stab at the satisfying record of his species. Like him, knowing that it is neither simple nor punishment free, I sniff out the archive of my history, that of Huns and Tatars, Lithuanians, Jews, and Byelorussians, Austrians and Prussians, all of whom have left their scent on that lamppost between Germany and Russia called Poland.

In that part of the world there is always struggle. If one looks at any two communities there, they are always at odds, always fighting between themselves, always crushed by a third. They try to play the third against the other, and they always lose. And there is always art. There, art is a weapon. I want to be in touch with that art, the life and death quality of that art. As I read the introduction to Zbigniew Herbert's book of poetry, *Report from a Besieged City*, I am stunned by two sentences. "The first edition of this book was published by internees of the Rakowiecka Prison in Warsaw in 1983. Almost all copies were confiscated." In prison? We're talking about poetry?

> *...how difficult it is to establish the names*
> *of all those who perished*
> *in the struggle with inhuman power*

the official statistics
reduce their number
once again pitilessly
they decimate those who have died a violent death
and their bodies disappear
in abysmal cellars
of huge police buildings

eyewitnesses
blinded by gas
deafened by salvoes
by fear and despair
are inclined toward exaggeration

accidental observers
give doubtful figures
accompanied by the shameful
word "about"

and yet in these matters
accuracy is essential
we must not be wrong
even by a single one

we are despite everything
the guardians of our brothers

ignorance about those who have disappeared
undermines the reality of the world . . .

In Poland there is always war, resistance, heroism. Even though I left when I was eight years old, I feel especially at home there. The place is still reliving the Second World War, my war, when Poland and I parted company. There are memorials everywhere, flowers left daily at certain street corners, commemorating another pocket of resistance, another group of heroes. In Poland, they commemorate September 1, the day the Germans began their invasion, and now even September 17, the day the Soviets began theirs. Both dates have a powerful resonance in my personal history.

In Poland, life is miserable, the stores are empty, the currency worthless, the air unbreathable, the water rusty and thick with deadly chemicals. Prospects are dismal, in spite of the onset of a free market economy or a return to democracy.

A man has saved his millions of zloty, carries them over to a car dealer to order a new Polish Fiat.

"You understand that delivery will be in ten years," the dealer informs him.

The man understands.

The dealer looks at the calendar. "That will be November 28, 1999," he says.

"Morning or afternoon?" the buyer asks.

The dealer is surprised, "Sir, what do you care? Delivery is a whole ten years away."

"Yes," says the buyer, "but in the morning the plumber is coming."

Pain and struggle exist everywhere, even in the midst of foliage season. We have our miseries here in Vermont, our homeless, our own brand of despair. Poland is not the only place where bigots thrive. Were Vermont not so lily-white, racism would undoubtedly be more apparent than it is. And anti-Semitism, as everywhere, is always poised to erupt.

Vermont is the source of art for some. For me, even when I painted, it was not. Nor is it usually the source of my writing. But people make art everywhere, art that instructs, enriches, makes life worthwhile. The need for distant sources, for cauldrons of pain and struggle, is mine, a personal need mired in the circumstances of my own life. It is my irresistible attraction, while realizing that we are all capable of making our prisons, our life and death struggle, anywhere we settle.

There is no denying that some art is born of silence and isolation, of the contemplation of nature, the abstract play of geometry or color. There is a sublime art of flowers, landscape, the erotic. None of this is born of war or chaos or tumult. A Zen master might well thrive in foliage season. Others of us do the best we can.

On Straightening a Curve in the Road

Norma Jane Skjold

A person probably shouldn't get so possessive about trees or about road frontage. After all, the trees would have died someday anyway, and the road, well, who knows what might yet happen to the road. There are no sure things, no permanent conditions, no utter absolutes in this life. I know that and I still regret all change.

The fact is, of course, that if I'd bought my place without trees, or with the road frontage already straightened, I'd never have noticed what might have been or what ought still to be. I'd be like any other new arrival, so impressed to be living in Vermont that I wouldn't notice the "improvements" that have so altered my private landscape.

If I was young again and had not yet married, or had never been widowed, or had yet to attend the funeral of a friend, death would also remain a hazy concept, not quite so close to home, not nearly as intrusive upon my own personal landscape as it has come to be. But that is a function of maturation, I suppose, to learn how much we don't control.

And I don't suppose the trees would have mattered so much either, if they hadn't gone down the very summer of the year of so many other losses. If they hadn't gotten cut, if the road hadn't been widened, and if that curve hadn't been straightened just when it was that year, then perhaps the whole project would not have taken on such a metaphorical flavor in my mind. As it is, though, the absence of those trees has become a very personal affront, and every day when I come home from work and see, once again, that they are missing, I am reminded of how much else is also gone. The selectmen could not have anticipated such an equation, of course, nor could the road crew have imagined the sorrow their chain saws perpetrated against my front yard.

To them this was simply one more stretch of road to make better, one more hill to improve for the school bus, and we who lived alongside it were simply "the landowners" whose approval or disapproval was immaterial, since the town already owned the right-of-way. And I would guess that someone probably told me, when my husband and I bought our house in Vermont, that the trees that provided such a welcome sense of enclosure stood outside the line that demarcated the limits of our ownership. I probably heard it, may have understood it, but didn't comprehend the threat contained within those simple facts.

Trees appear to be permanent, after all. One expects them to last at least as long as one's own lifetime, just as one expects one's husband and friends and neighbors to do. One does not suspect that such permanent-looking manifestations of life might disappear or be taken away without one's permission. One has rights, you understand. One has a piece of paper with signatures affixed to it, and there is ownership involved because of that; there is the ownership of assumptions. And for as long as one's life is untouched by catastrophe, those assumptions mutter along in a serviceable fashion, providing a kind of background of security. Afterward, however, nothing seems safe. I understand now how old-timers can miss current beauty in their regret about the loss of the past. I too have crossed that line between naive, enthusiastic youth and threatened old age, with almost no time at all in complacent middle age. It has nothing to do with years.

My husband was killed in a plane crash when we had just turned forty. My best friend had died of breast cancer a few years before, and another good friend died of breast cancer the year after. In the middle of it all, my neighbor across the road, who was only in his sixties, died of heart disease, and the summer after that, they tore down our trees and straightened the curve in the road.

Do you wonder that I have come to fixate on those trees? I have not gotten on another airplane since my husband was killed (though I have my own private pilot's license), and I get mammogram X-rays done every year since my women friends have died, and still, as you know, none of this touches the pain of the grief. Loss gets translated into fear of loss and no matter how one tries, one controls neither. Friends tell me I am more likely to die of worry than of cancer or accident at the rate I am going, and then we laugh and I come home and I see those missing trees.

I live on what is quite possibly the most beautiful hill in all of the Northeast. I'm told that everyone in Vermont feels this way. My little wood-heated cabin sits on a knoll halfway down a hill overlooking a great blue lake, and if I time my evening homecomings just right, I am treated to the most spectacular sunsets and rising mists and shadows anyone has ever imagined. On certain days it's like a Bierstadt painting, on others it's an impressionist watercolor. I have eased down that maple-lined hill in all seasons for the last ten or so years and have never seen the same light twice. I try sometimes to capture it in photographs, and if I miss, there is no second chance. There are only more variations.

My house, too, is quite likely the only house I will ever find that suits me as perfectly as it does. It was not inexpensive to buy, but it is cheap to keep. Its brick peasant stove and its passive solar windows and its heat-absorbing slate floors make it decidedly affordable, which is essential for a woman who is now living alone on women's wages in Vermont. And, given the way property values have tripled during the last several years, it is lucky that I do like my present shelter because I couldn't afford to buy another even if I did want to move, which I don't.

One of the first, last, and best rules of advice there is to read about bereavement is not to move. Stay still and heal, writes everyone who knows. Keep to familiar surroundings, make no changes in any of the matters over which one does still have some control, such as employment and routine, and wait for time to make even the most inconceivable thing, which is what death is, almost acceptable.

Therefore, I stay. Anyone else, with her road frontage summarily stripped of its screen of trees, would probably hammer a for-sale sign up on that denuded front lawn, but I haven't, and I won't, because I can't. This is where my husband left me when he died, and this is where I have faced down several years of night terrors, and this is where I feel—no matter how mistakenly—like I'm at home.

I'm not at home here, of course. Like a lot of the people who live in Vermont, I come from somewhere else. I come from a part of the country where trees do not grow unless you plant them and where shelterbelts are a prized feature of any homestead. I come from what is known as the high plains, which is another way of saying that it's flat and open to the wind and to the blizzards and tornadoes. My homeland is a natural prairie that gives protection only to those residents who can burrow underground. We who lived on top were exposed, and felt exposed, because out there, even in the hills, a person travels miles between trees.

Out there, in Nebraska, Arbor Day is taken seriously. When Halsey State Forest was burned in a prairie fire—which is the most terrible disaster one can face on the tinder-dry plains—every schoolchild in the state contributed money and time to replant the trees, because every schoolchild knows that in Nebraska, a tree is a treasure. Every schoolchild also knows that one does not burn one's ditches or one's stumps without plenty of water trucks standing by, and neither does one take any risks with sparks in the hay field or with cigarettes. Lightning can start a fire in a haystack and can burn one's entire hay crop, as well as one's fields and pastures and even one's cattle, if one is very unlucky, in a matter of hours.

Old-timers in the sandhills can tell about how one summer they were working in the hay fields when the whole sky turned dark, and neighbors from all around gathered up their cans of water and fire-fighting gear and trucked north toward where the clouds of ash were rising and where a fire was evidently burning out of control. It was only after they got to the banks of the Niobrara River, which runs between Nebraska and South Dakota, that they realized, to their great relief, that the fire they so feared was burning in the Black Hills several hundred miles to the north.

On good days, when the work was done enough to go for a drive, my husband and I, who lived for some years on my grandfather and great-grandfather's original homestead out there, would take off with another couple of neighbors to go look around at the miles and miles of grass-covered dunes in the sandhills for an afternoon. And no matter where we started out, we always ended up driving by what was one of the most amazing sights there was to see in that country—a great acreage of dark green pines, planted by a very determined old homesteader in the early days, in a fit of what was clearly a desperate case of homesickness for the forests of the East.

It was said that he carried water by team and wagon to those miles and miles of baby pines for years until they had finally sunk roots deep enough into the dunes to stand the hard life of that desert country on their own. Some said he did it in memory of a dead wife. It was, they said, a way to keep busy and to provide something living and green for generations to come. Others pointed out that homesteaders were, by law, required to plant shelterbelts on their 160-acre allotments of land in order to "hold" them against the wind and the elements and that Kincaiders, who were given land grants of 640 acres in the grassy dunes of the much poorer sandhills, sometimes went a little crazy trying to plant enough trees.

It was years before the sandhills, which is the greatest and largest inland desert in this hemisphere, even if it is grassed over, was discovered to be suitable only for cattle and not for farming. Native Americans could have told the settlers that, of course, but nobody asked the Sioux for their opinion as they pushed them farther and farther north to the reservations of the Badlands. Eventually, though, cattlemen came to notice that the buffalo they killed off had not been starving, and they began to build ranches.

I was raised on such a ranch, although not in the worst (or the best) of the sandhills, and my ancestors' homesteads were located north along the Niobrara River, which is an area of hills including a few dunes. There were giant cottonwood trees planted around the homesite where we lived, and there was a long shelterbelt, five rows deep, of other cottonwoods and cedars to the west of where we fed the cattle in the winter. We could not have stood it out there on those plains, either in the winter or the summer, without those trees. The cattle, most especially, could not have survived the terrible howling blizzards that blew through every winter without cedar trees and buck brush to back into.

To someone like me, who was raised to regard trees as living treasure, to love lakes, and to fear certain kinds of storm clouds as similar to a biblical holocaust, Vermont looks like paradise. Vermonters think of trees as a kind of pest, of course, and look at fields as places to keep cleared at considerable effort and expense, lest they go back to forest. I can only be astonished that any natural environment, left to its own devices, would choose forest.

Where I come from, the natural environment, left to its own devices, chooses to be prairie. Any "natural" stands of trees found in Nebraska are found only alongside streams or rivers or stock ponds and then only in a narrow strip, stamped bare underneath by the livestock.

I continue to be amazed, even after ten years, that the huge black storms that blow down from Canada into Vermont do not, as a rule, contain tornadoes and very seldom develop into pounding, frightening blizzards in the winter. I am endlessly pleased that the snow falls here in a gentle cover and does not pile up into drifts and does not, as a rule, threaten one's life the way it does on the plains. In Nebraska, if your vehicle goes off the road or stalls out on the way home, you are very likely to freeze to death either if you try to walk or if you stay put. The windchill is so bitter that you can die within sight of a farmhouse, and if you stay in your car, you run the risk that the road crews won't find you for some days, with all the miles of roads they have to clear. In Vermont, if your car goes off the road, you simply get out and walk the few hundred feet to any of several houses that are always nearby to call for help, or you wait for someone you know to drive by.

In Vermont, drought is a word people use for when there begins to be dust on the road in the summer; where I come from, drought is when the lakes and springs and ponds dry up and one has to sell cattle or watch them die. Where I come from, drought, like fire, is a real and present danger, and it occurs oftener than anyone cares to acknowledge.

By comparison, Vermont looks like a garden.

Now the boy who used to mow my lawn has been killed in a car crash. He was twenty-one. His father, who is often the Town Meeting moderator, was one of the selectmen who straightened the curve in the road that went between my land and the neighbor's farmyard several years ago. His father was also the one who listened the most when I regretted out loud the loss of my trees, and he hired a man to plant a single row of cedars as a kind of replacement, though the town was in no way obliged to placate me.

The little church in our village was packed to standing room only for the funeral. There were people on the stairs who couldn't get in, who had come to grieve that boy's death. The man who runs the sawmill, who is a lay minister and who delivers a lot of the eulogies that must be spoken for his neighbors, read most beautifully from the Scriptures and remembered the boy we were burying.

I became aware, in a way that is easy to forget, that I do in fact live within a community here. I do in fact have neighbors, and friends who are still living, who meet me for meals, who offer a kind of human shelterbelt against the buffetings of these many burials.

I have friends like that out West, as well, and I have family there, too, but I feel safer here, if only because of the weather, if only because of the rain and the trees and the lakes, and I have put down tentative, slow-growing roots in this cold and bony ground.

I may not ever transplant entirely, the way cactus does not do well in good soil, and I may never acclimate to the differing view of trees that prevails here, but at the very least, I will have used this time I have lived in Vermont to love lakes and mountains and civilized, protected pockets of human habitation.

I will have used this time to get accustomed, however unwillingly, to the fact and the idea of change.

Water

Howard Norman

If anything is clear in the Year of the Earthquake, Americans have an overblown sense of authority over their environment. Take water. In Vermont, why would I fully expect water to pour from every faucet, as if water, drawn up against gravity and running through a system of metal pipes, were part of the natural order, like moonlight or death? When I think of my eighteen months in an arctic village where a glacier was the looming reservoir, I realize how much we live at the mercy of our own contrivances. Once, driving home to Boston from Amherst along Route 2, fields covered with new snow, I was waved over by a man standing next to his Buick. The hood was up; the radiator hissed a geyser of steam. His wife sat glowering in the front seat. In the distance several huge crows whirled over a barn. "Can you bring us back some water?" he inquired, a note of cold impatience in his voice. I had seen two cars pass him by. At this point, in a strange conjunction of thought, we both turned and stared as if transfixed by sunlight glinting off perhaps a hundred acres of frozen water. "Sorry," he said, embarrassed. But I had not recognized the field of snow in any relation to the empty radiator, either. In my rearview, I saw him cupping snow in his hands. He appeared prayerful.

Disappointments are in direct relation to expectations. It is not so much that a water well, for example, may fail to work; it is that it may not work according to one's expectations of how, when, and to what degree of domestic convenience it *should* work. There are larger forces telling us that we do not deserve such successes, is my theory. I once observed a sixty-year-old Inuit man, Moses Nuqac, fashion a kayak over a period of ten or so days. It had a kinetic grace, a sleek sense of motion even on land. To my mind it was perfect; to ride in it would be an embrace, a protection from death in a realm where death invented ways to deal with people venturing out in kayaks. But to Moses' mind, practical wisdom was predicated not on the expert construction of the kayak but on the wider world. "It's a nicely built boat," he remarked, "but the sea is full of surprises." I may be remembering the last word inaccurately; he may have said "ambushes." Life as a whole is a cautionary tale. Moses had had three cousins and one uncle drown in kayaks—that is, flung from them, the uncle by a walrus—he had made. But, by extremely hard-earned consensus, he was the best kayak builder in the history of the village.

Speaking, though, of Vermont, archaeologists tell us that most of the earliest known western Abnaki Indian sites, in my general region of the state (East Calais; formerly Moscow), were typically located "near a supply of water." Of course this refers to lakes, rivers, creeks; in modern well digger's terminology, "surface water." As for water's subterranean hideouts, in the Abnaki language was a phrase I trust. It refers to water suddenly gurgling out of a crag (the "gurgling" part is important, as it implies water announcing itself) or hole: *water-came-up-because-it-wanted-to.*

A pause:

Freud told us that families, too, are contrivances. The *perfect* family, he said, is a contrivance of projected balances, idyllic associations drawn up from the subconscious by astonishingly willful flexings of the imagination. A perfect family, then, is a kind of powerful lie to the self. Reality—the actual family dynamic—is an altogether different beast. Last July, when our well went dry, my older brother ambushed me with phone calls. I will forever think of the two events as somehow inextricably bound up with each other.

Scott Bassage, our dear neighbor, brought over three garbage cans full of water on the bed of his truck. We set them on the back porch. My own family—myself; my wife, Jane; my thirteen-month-old daughter, Emma—needed a new well. We needed a new pump and pipeline, possibly a cistern. Our farmhouse is located on the south slope of Peck Hill Road, on about thirty-five acres.

It had been hot all summer. At 6:00 A.M., on the July day in question, the radio said that the temperature was seventy-four degrees and would climb to ninety degrees by noon. Shortly after six, the well diggers were encamped in my side yard, in front of the double shed. There were two—Jack, the foreman, and his assistant, Toby. They had towed an enormous drilling rig whose erector-set top was up among the maples. There was also an auxiliary water tank, primarily used to keep the rig lubricated. The company had "fit me in"; it was a bad year for water, good for drilling.

I made us coffee. I felt a bit ridiculous, carrying out three steaming cups on a tray—who was working for whom?—especially after noticing their workmen's thermoses and lunch pails. Truth was, deep down, my anxiety was beginning to rise. I can put it this way: I knew they were going to earn a lot of money, and this made me want to take their coffee back. I had already lost enthusiasm; the aesthetic pleasures of watching a well dug would come only in retrospect. According to the contract, the digging would cost $7.50 a foot. Lunch pails were menacing; lunch meant at least six hours of labor and I did not know how many feet per hour. We all stood near the rig, its ticking wall of gauges. The thing was warming up. Jack was about forty-five, a stocky man with an oddly chiseled face, one notch of which was a deep cleft in his chin. He had badly cut hair. He was dressed in a gray T-shirt, jeans, and mud boots. Quickly downing his coffee, he handed me the cup, then offered a smile of complicity, a smile that irked me. "Last week," Jack said, "we went just a hundred feet. A house not too far from here, either." His demographics were purposely vague. The location of underground pools was unpredictable. A "gusher" may be ten feet from a dry well or ten miles. Therefore, in terms of luck, proximity meant nothing. I truly regretted not hiring a water witch—it might have been interesting—though I had heard about their failures, too. To the believer, superstition has more practical import than any technology, perhaps simply because it is older. Anyway, Jack said what he said with professional optimism, which I rejected. Our very honest local journeyman, Ronnie Clark, told me about my neighbor's well. He said it was on a "wet hill," as opposed to my hill, a dry one. I stared out over the landscape, past our maples, stone fence, sloping field, then over to the barn that sequesters the house from highway noise. Jack noticed my brooding. "Look," he said, "this is Vermont, not the Mojave Desert." Then he went about his business. There was a loud growl and the rig cranked up; its spiral bit gnawed into the ground.

I went back inside. It was seven o'clock. In the kitchen, the noise was there, the grind and modulating pitch of the drill, a few disconnected words shouted out. Jane and Emma were still somehow asleep upstairs. I read the contract over again. It more or less stated that not finding water was an Act of God.

The telephone rang, a faint buzz in the distance that seemed farther than the pantry. The drilling was louder than I had imagined. I carried the phone into the corner of the pantry, shut the door.

"Hello?"

"It's me."

It was my brother, three years my elder, ten months out of federal prison in Indiana; mail fraud, tax evasion, the details were never available to me. I had not heard his voice in roughly two years. In his last letter from Terre Haute, he had mentioned being surrounded by ex-mayors and playing regular tennis. And that he was corresponding with a rabbi in Michigan. And cooking a thousand eggs a morning, in the "mess." When I pictured him as I had last seen him, at my youngest brother's wedding, I saw an overweight man whose every smallest gesture was a scheme. A man flashing clips of hundred dollar bills, impressing himself, if that. A man full of fear and heaviness of spirit, who, for some reason, seemed more like an uncle than a brother, a good-hearted uncle, perhaps, though one incapable of acting kind.

"Well, it is you."

"Know what I did yesterday?"

"Shot the sherrif? No—what?"

"I went to the Mulick Park swimming pool."

"You're back in Michigan?"

"The Great Lakes State."

"Why the pool?"

"The pool we learned to swim in as kids. I was ten. You were seven. I wanted to be shut of that pool, you know? I wanted to shut it out of my life."

"So you went to it?"

"I was driving around the old neighborhood there in Grand Rapids. I saw the diving board, the link fence—that did it. The sight of that fence. I went and bought a cheap swimsuit at Kreske's. I'm a size lower since prison. And I dove in. What pissed me off was—what got me angry all over again was right away I swallowed water. That chlorine taste. And it made me remember that you learned to swim faster than me, even though we took lessons at the same time and me being older."

"So what?"

"So what is, it's a bad memory, is what. A bad memory I have of you. You *knew* I was older, so you should've held back in your swimming so as not to humiliate me."

"Is that why you called, to say this?"

"I'm your brother, I need a reason?"

"Usually you have one."

"What's that noise in the background?"

"They're digging a well. We bought a farmhouse here. It's our first summer in it."

"Look buddy, I haven't been getting bulletins on your life. I just heard you were in Vermont. I got the number from information, like any normal citizen. They give out phone numbers, they don't say anything whether it's a fucking *farm*house or a fucking *out*house. My big shot brother the landowner, with his farmhouse."

"It's not like that. It's a typical mortgage situation."

"Well, let me inform you something. I don't own anything. But I can go back to my motel room and stick my face under the bathroom faucet, turn the water on all day if I want. I can *drown* in it." He slammed down the phone.

I brought breakfast up to Jane and Emma. Emma had her face pressed to the guest room window, watching the well diggers. The noise upset her, but she also seemed mesmerized—the rig hovering up two stories. I decided to drive to the market a quarter mile away, Legares. Out on Route 14. At the market I bought eggs, apples, pears, plums, grapes, a normal day. Returning back around the curve, I looked off to my left and saw the top of the rig, unnatural, out of place. It towered there the way you might see a giraffe's head and neck in the distance, when you enter the gates of a zoo. Driving up, I found six men on my lawn. There were Toby and Jack, my neighbor Maurice Persons, the local road commissioner, and two others I had never seen before or at least did not recognize. Amidst the grinding noise I received looks of sympathy all around. Obviously the loss of water brings a kind of grief. Now this group was holding a temporary vigil. "I heard you had water problems," the road commissioner said, shaking my hand. The yard was torn up. Toby had dug a thin, shallow gulley through which sludge thick as cement and a similar color runnelled into the backyard, with a tributary into the small flower garden. Toby was delicately hoeing the sludge along as though herding sheep through a sluice gate into a pen. Jack checked the gauges, which he did every three or four minutes; they relayed news from underground. Toby now had an apple in his mouth and was eating it without using his hands. "When we were at 150," Jack shouts, "we had some water, but it was surface water, we call it, and it came out good and clear but then it was gone. Even if there's eighty gallons a minute, if it's not clear, it's a bad well. We're into the kind of rock we like to see, though. But you don't have a well yet." From the sludge, Toby walked over to contribute a fact. "Deepest we've ever gone is 620," he says. And I believe he means this as a limit to how deep they would ever go and how deep they once had to go. In my darkening mood I take it as self-fulfilling prophecy.

Jane is shouting from the side porch, holding her hand to her ear: the telephone. Tracking in mud, I watch her head upstairs with lunch.

"Hello?"

"Still in Michigan."

"Good for you."

"Have you by the way looked at a map of Vermont lately? For your benefit I bought one."

"Your calls are collect; you live in a motel without phones in the room?"

"Vermont, according to this map, is full of lakes. There's a lake every quarter inch or so. How can you be out of water?"

"Technically speaking, lakes are surface water."

"Get off it—people *drown* in lakes. Deep under them. Tell me nobody's. . ., you're telling me Lake Champlain is surface water? I think you're getting screwed, is my opinion. You've come there from the city, my friend. You don't think that the people digging your well can't see a *killing*? You think Vermont is the paradise of human behavior? Stop the drilling, I'll visit. I'll supervise for you. That's my offer, here and now, in return. One thing I didn't tell you, is that I learned some plumbing in Indiana. A well is just *plumbing*. I'll supervise."

"There's already a supervisor."

"I was probably in the can with him."

He hangs up.

Hidden in the pantry I make a few calls designed to temper my apprehension, which it turns out they do not. I call Andy Potok in his quiet office, who tells me the cost of the well he'd had put in the previous winter. "But our water's gushing like Old Faithful," he adds. I call Ed Koren in Brookfield, who is not home. Curtis, his wife, says they are out of water and that Ed has been lugging a supply up from the village. I call Bill Tekosky at Rainbow Sweets Bakery. "Want to take a shower at our house?" he offers.

I hang up; the phone rings.

"You were on the phone," my brother says, his tone fashioning the obvious into an indictment.

"I was talking to some friends."

"Good for you. You and your *friends*. You're there sucking water from your dishwasher drain and what're your so-called friends doing on your behalf? You and your friends, terrific."

"What did you mean, 'in return'?"

"What?"

"You said, you'd come supervise the well in return. Return for what?"

"Since you asked. My situation needs help. I've fallen into a bind. I'm in some difficulty, in terms of the law. Being in Vermont you can be of direct..."

"...assistance, I bet. Just how is that?"

"According to my map Vermont has a Canadian border close by."

"So does the whole country."

"Your house...excuse me, farmhouse. It's in Vermont, is what I'm saying. You're my brother. You have a daughter I haven't seen. My niece. In a nutshell, here's my offer. I come and visit, soon. Then, after a few days of quality time with my niece you drive me one night into Canada. That way I'll fall out of my bind."

"That's your offer."

"I see you need time to think it over. Stay off the phone, will you?"

Almost at three o'clock, the insatiable rig plummeting, and there is a drizzling rain. It takes back-to-back hours of steady rain soaking into the ground to fill a well. Raincoat on, I measure the old well by dropping a flat stone on the end of a thread, then measuring the thread. "We just drop a stone down," Jack says, close up. "Time it with a regular second hand." The old well is only one-half inch higher. Besides, its pump has probably been struck by lightning. It is a miserable afternoon. The well diggers are bivouacked under a hand-held tarpaulin. "We're at 330 now," Jack says. "We'll go till six, maybe seven o'clock if we have to, then come back in the morning." Inside, Jane has left a cheerless note on the kitchen table: "3:30—Handel's *Water Music*. WGBH." At the top of the stairs, I see Jane and Emma napping in the big bed. The rain on the roof with its soporific cadence. There is no greater contrast, I think, than my anxiety over water and the sweet, deep afternoon's sleep in our bedroom, from which through my own volition I am an exile.

"Hello?"

"I need to get to Canada. I saw a suspicious car in the motel parking lot. A man got out. There were binoculars on the seat."

"You're having a paranoid delusion. What'd you do—was it federal again?"

"Let's just say it was something Canada could help me with."

"Here's the position you put me in, not to mention that I don't hear from you for two years."

"For which you could thank me. Besides, you've heard from me so much already this summer."

"That's as follows: I'm here, Jane and the baby are here. And you want me to be an accomplice, is the word. To drive a federal offense person..."

"Your brother."

"...into Canada. What, lying in the trunk?"

"*Jerk*, answer me this. Am I a brother or a 'federal offense person'?"

"Both, apparently."

"There's places to cross, not through an official spot. All sorts of back roads. Even a field, a house where a yard ends...two steps, into another country."

"You've got movies in your head."

"Here's my offer. One: I visit. Two: The kid has quality time with her uncle. Three: We all have a little picnic about a hundred miles north of your farmhouse. Little Emma points and says, 'Dadda, what's that?' And you being such a good Dadda, says, 'Why, that's Canada, honey. Where your uncle's going to live.' We make it a family occasion. Four: I give you permission, officially on paper and signed, to use the whole incident in a novel. There's a lot in this offer. You'd be surprised how much I'm offering here."

Stifling heat at five o'clock in the afternoon. I'm looking out the living room window and see Toby strip off his shirt. The rain has stopped. He walks to the auxiliary tank on the flatbed truck. On the side is a spigot. Toby reaches into his pocket, finally producing a small plastic container that he empties onto his head. It is shampoo. He vigorously scrubs his hair, drying it with a towel after a long rinse. He combs his hair back in a fifties duck's ass style.

Jack appears in the open kitchen doorway. "We're at 460 now. The rock is soaked, but we're measuring only three-quarters gallon a minute. It's costing, I know, but it's not a well yet. We can do better for you."

The-water-did-not-come-up-because-it-did-not-want-to.

I do not sleep all night, lying in the guest room away from Jane and Emma sound asleep in their separate beds. Two or three times I walk outside barefooted and listen down the shaft, a faint whisper like listening to a seashell. I do not feel fit for sleeping or being slept next to. At 6:30 A.M., I watch the well diggers return. I walk to Bassage's corncrib—converted into an office—and start a letter, then fall asleep. Walking back, I find the rig is gone, vanished. Jack is waiting for me next to his pickup. "We got about five gallons a minute—at 605. Probably what'll happen is that where we've cracked rock it'll shift and open things up down there even more. You can listen down into it now and hear water pouring in."

We shake hands. "Hey—your phone's ringing," he says.

I think I have never felt so tired in my life.

"Hello?"

"You know what's *weird*?" my brother says. "Whenever I try talking sense to you, I get parched. This amazing thirst. When I hang up I'll probably require ten glasses of water in a row. It's a true mystery. Why do you think that is? Have you thought over my offer of that picnic?"

We Are All Farmers

Frank Bryan

There is, in a certain valley in southern Vermont, the quintessential Vermont farmscape—flowing meadows, a meandering brook, huge maples working their way up the adjacent ridges. If there is better potential for a *Vermont Life* cover anywhere between New York and New Hampshire, where it is I don't know.

But when you drive round the bend, what do you see? Trash.

The ungodliest, ugliest panorama of crap on God's green earth. There is a barnyard fenced in with junk cars; literally, the cars are the fence. The barn is falling down, saved only by long poles jammed in the ground and leaning against its walls. Dead tractors, broken fences, bygone refrigerators, and other household items lie scattered. Most are used for spare parts. Others are used for storage. Imagine the tackiest lawn adornment you've ever seen. It's there. Imagine generations of personal paraphernalia stored, not in the attic but outside. It's awful.

Bear in mind this is no figment of my imagination. It's a real place occupied by a man we can call (to protect him from a lynch mob of Vermont's pretty people armed with bureaucratic decrees) Farmer Brown.

I say, Hooray for Farmer Brown.

You are, the saying goes, what you eat. Similarly, a state is what its people are. Thus, Vermont is not its scenery. Yet despite its hardscrabble geography, Vermont is more and more becoming a place that can be shaped by the way its people live. And it is precisely because people are becoming more and more capable of bulldozing the character of the land into grotesque and even dangerous shapes and forms that Vermont now faces the agonizing dilemma of meshing the contradictory concepts of freedom and planning. It is also why the most critical decisions we must make involve politics, the way in which we do this.

What if we kept Vermont but lost the Vermonters? There seems to be great consensus about what we want Vermont to look like. But do we know what we want Vermont to be?

Blowing in the wind over the passing of the twentieth century, these questions seem as elusive to the great portion of Vermont's ruling class (and we do have one) as dandelion puffs in the breezes of May. Since these questions will define Vermont for a century to come, the first thing to do is to face up to them. What to do with Farmer Brown? Or what about Bucky Cole?

Bucky was walking down a country road in Pomfret last November as the sun unsuccessfully tried to warm the bleak of a dying afternoon from behind a rolling bank of gray clouds. But, rifle slung over his shoulder, Bucky Cole's heart was happy. He hadn't seen any deer—every year these hills of his childhood produced fewer and fewer—but it didn't matter as much as it once did. Home was up the road, and there was no reason to be particularly alert even in the "prime time" of approaching dusk because most of the land was posted with "No Hunting" signs on both sides of the road.

Bucky lived in a trailer on fifteen acres of land his grandmother, May Cole, had given each of her children and grandchildren when she was about seventy-five. Until she was eighty-nine, she got in her Scout every day and drove down to the senior citizens center in Woodstock to help out. Radiating out from May Cole in great flowing ripples of life and community and home are fifty-six grandchildren and twenty-two great grandchildren.

The first time I ever saw May Cole, she was sixty-one and standing in the doorway of the milk room of her 200-acre hill farm. That was in the summer of 1962. Her husband had died years earlier, but she still kept the place going. Kept the cattle on the land and they, then, kept the land open. She and thousands like her in their sweat and their pain, in their frustration and in their hope, were the Vermont of hill and dale we love so much. They crafted and preserved the beauty we adore and covet today. They did it through the artistry of their work. Their canvas was the land. Their brush their calloused hands.

May had just finished chores and I had come to help her hay. She worked that day like a young man. Today, at ninety-three, May Cole lives alone in the little wooden house under the hill on five acres she kept for herself. Bucky lives just up the hill. One hundred yards to the north is Mildred's house, Bucky's mother. One hundred yards to the south is Bucky's brother's place. His name is Duffer.

Bucky graduated from Woodstock High School. During school days, he worked for Dave Moore, who built organs in a shop down the hill. Bucky became a talented craftsman and stayed on with Dave after graduation and became his foreman. If you are ever in the Grace Episcopal Church in Georgetown, the organ there was built and installed by Bucky Cole in 1978 when Dave sent him down to do the job.

Bucky's hobby is raising oxen and competing in ox draws in fairs around Vermont. At the time he kept nine of them and other cattle on the pastures of his grandmother's place. He didn't make any money in the ox business. He just loved it. And the people who went to the fairs loved it too—especially the newcomers flooding into Vermont. He sensed they respected the traditions he was hanging on to.

When he was twenty-nine, Bucky was elected president of the New England Ox Teamsters Association. He built a new barn and a cozy workshop where he made yokes and bows. He installed his own sawmill up across the road. Then he quit Dave and began to do contract work on his own. He now works as a finish cabinetmaker for a company in Lebanon, New Hampshire.

Like many kids, Bucky grew up in the working class—poor by most people's definitions. Not by his definition or mine, but by most folks'. Certainly nearly all those "from away" who are moving into Pomfret so rapidly see people like the Coles of Pomfret as belonging to a different "class."

Bucky was raised tough, too. He grew up within a huge extended family of tough men and women. They were men—as

Ansel Adams once said of true western cowboys "with the bark on" — and they were the kind of women who could handle that kind of man.

Two years ago, Bucky married, and he and his wife were carried from the church to the reception in a beautifully decorated cart drawn by Fred and Barney, his largest team; he had raised and trained them himself.

Bucky Cole is a Vermont success story. Raised in the hills, taking up a trade, contributing to his community — the kind of man who will stop and help you out of a ditch when you're stuck. Quiet of tongue. Gentle of spirit. Sharp and reasonable of mind.

That particular November day as he walked home along the road of his younger years, surrounded by the hills and valleys that had fashioned him, he was accosted by a middle-aged man who had hurried out of his house in his short sleeves.

"What are you doing out here with that gun?"

"Going home."

"Don't you know all this land is posted?"

"Yes."

"You know you can't hunt around here, don't you?"

"Yes."

"Well see to it that you don't. There's no hunting around here anymore, you know."

"I'm just walking home. I'm not hunting."

"Good."

The man turned on his heel and hurried back toward the house. Then a final thought stopped him. He stopped and shot it back in Bucky's direction. "Maybe you get a thrill out of running around here with those damn guns and killing innocent creatures. But we don't. We're going to put a stop to you and your friends."

Bucky told me this story while we ate breakfast in a little diner before heading up into the hills of Canaan, Vermont, deer hunting in the fall of 1989. He told the story with a wane, almost apologetic smile. He was embarrassed even in the telling. Not because he was wrong but because he had suffered a certain loss of dignity. Bucky's real hurt came from the way the man treated him.

"They think we're dirt," he said.

Bucky never made the standard complaints. He never articulated the incredible variety and range of atrocities for which this
one act of unthinking hostility stood as a profound metaphor.
He didn't whine. But although the exchange with the man had
taken place two years earlier, it still smarted. For he was telling
me he was not wanted at home anymore. He was being told that
his kind was not wanted in Pomfret. I looked in his eyes and I
saw Wounded Knee.

But Bucky's big sin in Pomfret was not deer hunting. It was
putting his trailer on a "ridge line" where it could be seen from
the picture windows of the newcomers', who had bought up surrounding property, houses. There is no one in Vermont—not even
the most ardent planner—who, if they heard the full story of
Bucky Cole's fight to build a home for his wife and his children
overlooking the dreams of his youth—the legal, administrative,
and political nightmare of it all—would not be horrified.

I have before me the July 1989 issue of *Vermont's Future*,
published by the Department of Community Affairs. In it is the
headline "Pomfret Ridgeline and Hillside Zoning Law." The accompanying article touts Pomfret's new bylaw that can deny a building
permit if it "interferes with the visual features of the landscape,
as viewed from a public highway." A picture is included and with
it the caption "Pomfret, Vermont, acts to protect its scenic hill-
sides." The regulatory paraphernalia designed to inhibit macro-
developers had instead ended up shafting another Vermonter. And
they almost succeeded.

"I was about ready to move out," said Bucky. "I guess us
woodchucks aren't very scenic."

We both laughed. Sort of. Then we went up on the Norton
Road and chased a big track in the snow until dusk.

I have a question. Why doesn't Vermont protect people like
Bucky Cole? It is their cattle, after all, that have helped keep
the pastures clear. They are the people that fashioned those hill-
sides in the first place. For those people that don't like looking
at people like Bucky Cole, I have this to say: You are more than
uncaring, elitist snobs. You are damned fools. Because without
Bucky, there can be no Vermont, no matter what the landscape
looks like.

Picture briefly a Currier and Ives print of Vermont. Such a vision is very much an approximation of the goals of Vermont's Act 200 statewide planning law. This is the law that was passed to control growth in Vermont by the institution of thirty-two statewide goals. How dear to my heart those goals and that picture is. Village and farm, green space and clustered communities. The image of Vermont painted by the Commission on Vermont's Future is precisely in sync with the memory of my youth, growing up green in the little Connecticut River valley town of Newbury. I read the commission's report, and the memories it conjures up take me back to the pastures of yesteryear and a mist of longing captures my heart. To be once again young in a village where the lowing of cattle and the cry of twilight whippoorwills was as natural as waking in the morning and falling asleep at night.

Then why does the Act 200 process, the political system put in place to give us a chance to realize our dreams of a clean, village-town, farm-dotted landscape, turn my stomach? Why does one who has fought his entire adult life to save the very culture the state planners now promote with such religious zeal become so profoundly disheartened by Act 200's blueprint for reform? In this question lies the crisis of Vermont politics as we face the last decade of the century.

This crisis features three words: language, perspective, and democracy. Its solution must deal with the disjunction between what Vermont is and what Vermont looks like. It cannot be reached unless we return again to the rooted values, the guts, of what it was that gave our forebears the courage to build Vermont in the first place. Among those values are a certain respect for, and fairness with, the culture of locality; an appreciation of the value of variety in human affairs—without which, indeed, there would be no art, no literature, no passion at all in the human soul; and, most important, an understanding of the nexus between the land that sustains the people and the people who sustain the land. For there is one truth that must once again be realized if Vermont, indeed, if the planet itself, is to be saved: We are all farmers, from those who till the soil to those who hire others to do it for them. Even the most committed condo dweller, to whom mowing the grass by the doorstep is a chore to be contracted away, depends ultimately on an earth that breathes.

Recently, editors of the *Rutland Herald* penned an editorial calling me an "ultraconservative." Strange, I thought, surely by social status I am no conservative. I was raised in a one-store town by my mother, who didn't even own a car. There were seven of us in my graduating class from Newbury High. Currently I own five Chevy Chevettes. I bought the first because it was the least expensive car I could find. Two I operate and the other three junks I use for parts. I own not one share of stock and only one suit, which I use for rare dress up. I voted for Vermont's ERA, oppose the death penalty, and don't approve the overturning of *Rowe vs. Wade.* In Vermont's congressional race I voted for Progressive candidate Bernard Sanders. Conservative? Ultraconservative? Jeezum Crow.

I am called a conservative, I guess, because I favor the conservation of both the landscape and the culture that built it. I am in love not only with Vermont the land but also with Vermonters and see no way to distinugish the two. I opposed Interstate 91. I think we ought to keep and strengthen Town Meeting. I favor little schools, slow roads, democratic government. I was appalled at the "Vermont, the Beckoning Country" campaign that fueled the growth revolution that began in the mid-1960s. When I went to college, the students on my floor called me "the farmer" even though I wasn't raised on a farm. It was not, in those days, a compliment.

In 1936 Vermonters went to Town Meeting as usual. As usual the meetings took from two to six hours. But it was not just business as usual that day. By the time they went home, those folks had accomplished more to save Vermont and its environment than has ever been done before or since. They did it in one fell swoop, and they did it democratically because their leaders trusted them.

In a statewide Town Meeting referendum, they voted down a massive Massachusetts-to-Canada federal highway planned for the crest line of the Green Mountains. I said crest line. Ninety percent above the 2,500-foot level. You want to talk environmental disasters? You want to talk growth at any cost? Read the debates on the Green Mountain Parkway issue. No issue in this century has caused more fervor in Vermont.

The late Ralph Nading Hill, the most eloquent chronicler of Vermont's past, described the parkway's defeat simply and well. Vermonters decided, he said, that their mountains "would not be hitched together." The hitching together of Vermont's mountains — at the top—by asphalt—would have destroyed them forever. Show me a politician today that would suggest such a thing and I'll show you a lunatic.

Lesson? Those who did the saving of Vermont in those days were called conservatives. When Vermonters in their wisdom chose to protect the sanctity and the loneliness of their distant hilltops from the dynamite and the bulldozers of that time, it was viewed by progressives as just another example of Vermont backwardness, of Yankee neanderthalism, a reactionary thrust against the inevitable progress and growth that all clear-thinking people accept and welcome.

Right.

Vermont's bottle ban is another example. About ten years ago I was giving a talk in southern Vermont and mentioned Vermont's first-in-the-nation ban against nonreturnable bottles. A lady from the audience corrected me saying Vermont wasn't the first because when she got here in the early 1970s, Vermont didn't have one but Oregon did.

There it is. Perspective. Or lack of it. Vermont repealed its first-in-the-nation bottle ban in the early 1960s. Why? Because progressives thought it anachronistic and bad for business. Those who opposed the repeal of Vermont's early bottle ban were called conservatives, of course. In the mid-1970s, spurred by progressive ideas like a concern for the environment, we reinstated it.

At the time of the first bottle ban, my interest in the ban was strictly economic. A bike ride (old red wagon lurching along behind at the end of a clothesline rope) along Route 5 in the spring after the snow melted but before the farmers did spring work would net big dough in those days.

Or take Interstate 91. To oppose that in the 1960s was to be really conservative. Maybe even ultraconservative. I opposed the extension from White River Junction, north up through the

Northeast Kingdom. But to no avail. The interstate was finished before the environmental revolution hit. Is there any doubt that if such a road were suggested today there would be massive opposition to it? Picture an interstate-less kingdom. Picture Route 5 meandering as it always has up the river north of Norwich, through the little towns and villages, alongside the farms. Picture a trip north up to St. Johnsbury and onward to Orleans, Coventry, and Newport; slow bends and strawberry stands. Cattle steaming in barnyards in February. Children in school yards. Country stores. Hitchhikers. The inevitable (and hilarious) "thickly settled" road signs warning there approaches an area of more than two houses. Picture that kind of road and only that kind of road in place now. To me, the ultraconservative, it is an appealing picture because with I-91 barreling its way up the valley, I am too apt to look at the kingdom and imagine a future Chittenden County. And the hell of it is that to the progressives of the day, the kingdom sans I-91 is an appealing picture, too.

That I am called ultraconservative doesn't matter one whit because I don't matter. But the fact that we have no political language even to describe the dimensions of the most important political debate of our time matters plenty. It matters not only for the limitations it places on the political process but also for what it says about our lack of awareness of our own history, of our frightful present mindedness, of our incapacity to harvest lessons from the fertile bottomland of our own experience.

Look, Vermont is a land not only of hardscrabble, irascible, liberty-loving, hard-core individualists, it is also a land of people who have put up with these kinds of folks. It is a land of people — some like Bucky Cole, some like Farmer Brown, most others like you and me — who let people live differently. The landscape these "conservatives" (language anyone?) created and have protected so well (perspective, please) was grounded on democracy and nurtured by the mixing of life on a hard land and the character of those who survive it.

The result is Vermont's special brand of communalism. Land-based societies tend to democracy because nature teaches that liberty is essential and democracy (human scale and direct) is the only way to protect liberty in the context of yet another impulse nature inspires—coming in out of the cold, joining in social enterprise to fulfill the desire in our breast for comradeship. Can anyone who has stood alone on a hilltop in October when the hills are so beautiful it hurts deny it? The dominant emotions are a combination of the awe of Vermont's beauty and the longing to share it.

There is only one way to protect Vermont and that is to let Vermonters live out their lives democratically. Vermont must have room for the Farmer Browns. Most of Vermont's communities, if they are allowed, will do the right thing. But once in a while we'll turn a bend in the road and there they will be, basking in the ugliness of their own brand of orneriness, a glorious indecent gesture raised on high in the direction of all of us who don't like pink bathtubs on the front lawn or flower gardens made of old tractor tires. But Vermont is not Vermont in spite of Farmer Brown. It is Vermont because of him.

I've spent my adult life looking New Jersey right in the eye, watching it destroy my fishing holes, contaminate my hunting ground, throwing up "No Trespassing" signs on the vistas of my childhood. I've seen its agents insult my friends, herd many of them into trailer parks, berate them for their parochialism, zone away their backyards, make their farms unprofitable. I've stood beside the road as a kid hitching in the 1950s and had their ski-toting cars splash mud and slush all over my good pants. I've paid my dues. I've sweat my ass off in hay fields summer on summer and frozen my fingers filing a chain saw at twenty below in woodlots in December. I began working for the state geologist at sixteen in 1957—a sophomore in high school, boarding out in Peacham. The next year Vergennes. The next, Newport. I walked most of Vermont before 1960 and saw New Jersey on the horizon the whole time. I began my own personal efforts to save it with a letter to the editor in 1962. Ever since then, I've been called a conservative jackass for doing it. Still am.

I've watched the agents of progress destroy our schools, speed up our highways, "efficiency" our democracy out of existence. I've seen old Vermonters scoffed at and insulted and, worst of all, victimized by the soft smile of condescension that says: "You poor fool, you don't know how miserable you are. If only you had the brains to let us help you."

I've seen something else, too. I've seen the Vermont way of life become so stylized and cosmeticized that those of us who cling to it are accused of playing roles. My colleagues at the University of Vermont believe I live like I do down here in Starksboro to "prove a point." What an insult—the assumption that a Vermont life-style could not have an inherent value worthy of preservation for its own sake—that the urban model is the constant and any deviation from it must be artificial. I don't accuse urbanites of faking their urbanity. Why can't I be real, too? Why can't Vermonters be real? Why, in fact, can't they just be let be?

I've seen New Jersey all right. I've seen it coming for a lifetime, and by fighting it, I've been cast in the minority. But I've learned something. Most of those people who now at this late date have shown up to "save" Vermont have little appreciation for what Vermont is. They want, for instance, to save the farms. But I doubt they like (really like) farmers. The Speaker of the Vermont House of Representatives once said, "I've never been near a cow or a deer and I never want to either." At least he's honest.

There ought to be a law in Vermont. No one gets to "plan" Vermont until they've lived here for ten years. Anyone who believes you can understand Vermont without suffering (yes, suffering) through ten Aprils, end to end, doesn't know nature, can't understand that special relationship between the land and its people that stand behind the Vermont character, and won't be able to preserve the environment or the people who depend on it.

Color the perfect Vermont. Color every community planned, every roadway clean. Color the pastures preserved, the hilltops pure. Color the junk cars gone. (Color the trailer parks gone, too.) Then take away Vermonters.

Whatta ya got?

Nothin'.

Vermont's new statewide planning evangelists are good people. And they've got the vision of Vermont's landscape about right. But they've forgotten Farmer Brown and Bucky Cole. They just don't understand the symbiosis of land and character, of hills and people, and the strength the bond between them creates. They have forgotten that farmers are by nature feisty and that liberty is as essential to the Vermont landscape as farmland.

There is no way to keep Vermont Vermont without allowing for that certain feistiness and independence that a long-term personal relationship with the land and its creatures generates. And the only way to preserve that is to preserve Vermont's democracy.

In the meantime, I'm going to keep my eye on that little valley where Farmer Brown stands with his middle finger poised symbolically at those funny little cars that drive by with the out-of-state plates. And I'm going to keep my eye on Bucky Cole on his hilltop in Pomfret. As long as they stay rooted, Vermont is safe.

Midmorning Break

Alex Wilson

I watch Lillian push her little toy bulldozer over the sand embankment—where the full-size bulldozer scratched away the hillside a couple months earlier. Her Tonka plows through the soft sand, steering between plastic shovels, toy tractor, kitchen implements, and some wayward zucchinis from the garden—it's been one of those years when the zucchinis just got away from us; Jerelyn and I joke about taking the .22 out to the garden to do in the burgeoning squash before they block access to the garden. With the work on our new building and Frances having arrived in July, the garden simply lost out this year.

Lillian plays contentedly, laughing, talking to herself, her hair reflecting gold from the morning sun. A gentle breeze ruffles the summer dress that, with three-year-old stubbornness, she insisted on wearing for the morning's excavation work. I stand there watching her, taking another break from my writing despite (or perhaps because of) another looming deadline. I think about how relaxed she is playing in the sand, creating in her mind little adventures and games. She has no article deadlines to meet, no worries about whether the check will arrive in time to pay the health insurance premium, or whether the loan for a new printer will be approved.

I let my mind drift further—avoiding for a few more minutes my beckoning keyboard and research notes. How wonderful to be so unencumbered, so unaware of the problems faced by society. How nice it would be if poverty, toxic waste, nuclear proliferation, and the scores of other headline-grabbing problems facing our world did not have meaning for us—as they do not for Lillian. She has not yet heard of acid rain or ozone depletion. It will be at least several years before she learns about the theory that greenhouse gases spewed into the atmosphere by us may be elevating the Earth's temperature—by then the evidence of global warming may be undeniable by even the best, and highest-paid, industry lobbyist.

Most of our society is a lot like my three-year-old daughter, happily immersed in ignorance. Unaware and uncaring. We lead our lives with little if any realization of how we may be affecting the people around us, the air we breathe, and the earth that sustains us. Indeed, the motivation to remain ignorant is strong. To provide just for our own needs and comforts while wearing blinders to the ills of the world is a compelling life philosophy, one that is easy to accept. But it is also what gets us into trouble—failing to look out for our neighbors and our common environment. Will Lillian be any different as she grows up and learns more and more about how the real world operates?

When I write about environmental problems and measures we can take to solve them, I often find myself using Lillian as a reference. Can my efforts—and the efforts of many other like-minded individuals—help Lillian and her generation recognize and finally deal with these problems? I think so, I really do, especially when I look at how far we have come even in the last few years. The environment has moved back onto the agenda. It has even become the focus of advertising campaigns, touting this product or that as the one to buy if you want a clean environment. Imagine that! With concerns about the environment influencing consumer buying habits, we're just one step away from reaching corporate boardrooms and corporate policies. Then we will truly have come a long way.

The idea that consumers can make a difference was on my mind last winter when I began planning a new building—now a nearly enclosed shell. I had certain goals in mind for my twenty-four-by-thirty-two-foot garage and office building. Of course I wanted adequate space and comfort and a nice view of the orchard I put in eight years ago. But I had broader goals in mind as well. Because I write about building technology, energy, and the environment,

Midmorning Break   85

I wanted to make a statement—to myself, at least—about the right way to build. I wanted a building that would have a minimum impact on the environment: that wouldn't spew ozone-depleting CFCs (chlorofluorocarbons) into the atmosphere, that wouldn't encourage clear-cutting of the last remaining stands of virgin red cedar in the Pacific Northwest, that wouldn't consume too much fossil fuel—with its nefarious by-products—for heating.

Right away I ruled out rigid foam insulation containing CFCs—really the number-one environmental bad guy among construction materials. I'd get my insulation from thicker walls with cavity-fill insulation. I chose a new type of "wet-spray" cellulose insulation for the walls that's made from recycled newspaper and is thus helping to solve our solid waste woes. I chose native pine siding, which helps support the local economy, over plywood or wafer-board that is trucked here from thousands of miles away. I selected the most energy-efficient windows available—high-tech units with a thin metal coating to reflect outgoing heat radiation and argon gas between the layers of glass instead of air to boost its insulating value even more; my inch-thick windows will insulate better than the same thickness of fiberglass insulation. I planned the light fixtures so I could make use of the new compact fluorescent lights that consume one-fourth as much electricity as regular incandescent bulbs.

Because I don't have unlimited funds, I have to plan carefully. By spending extra money on better windows I must cut back on how much I can spend on labor—which means doing a lot of it myself. But that's all right, too. When I first went out on my own as a writer five years ago, I had to supplement my income by doing some carpentry work on the side. It was a nice mix: two days banging nails and three days writing. Because I write about building, I became a better writer by becoming a better builder. As I became more successful writing, however, I cut back on, and then eliminated, my construction work. This building is giving me a chance to get back into it and helping me realize how important a balance between physical and mental pursuits is in my life.

And I don't think I'm alone in my need for a healthier balance. It's a problem throughout our society. Our legislators developing farm policy in Washington might do a better job if they spent some of their Monday mornings behind the wheel of a tractor instead of behind the same old desk laden with piles of reports. Physicians might cope better with the high-pressure nature of their work if it was interspersed with lengthy interludes of something totally different—if I were a doctor, I think I'd want to balance it with something solid and solitary like dry-stone masonry, where mistakes aren't quite as critical and patients less likely to sue if the repairs fail. Teachers, too, could use more balance in their lives. Many of our teachers have never experienced life on the other side of those brick walls; they jump right back into the classroom after finally getting out of one themselves, never having gotten a different perspective on life. Perhaps we should encourage teaching as a second career—built on a foundation of real-life experience. Perhaps that would help to generate enthusiasm in the classroom, which we so desperately need.

In fact, I've often thought about becoming a teacher myself someday. With every article or installation manual I write I learn a lot—not only about the issue at hand but about the process of working efficiently as well. Maybe once I get tired of dealing with tight deadlines, telephone answering machines, and overnight mail, I'll be ready to settle down and share with others what I've learned. Maybe our society would do well to shift in that direction—sort of like the old master craftsman/apprentice relationship.

For the near-term, I think the ideal balance would be something like three quarters of my time writing and the other quarter working with my hands: either farming, building, or cabinetmaking. If I could succeed in working it out so as to provide a real separation, that would indeed be a very satisfying life-style—and I think it would make me a better writer.

As I lean back against the old maple tree, resting my eyes on the ever-more-real building, all the philosophical justifications of building material choices and all the thoughts of a better balance to life fade into the background. I picture myself spreading out in the spacious main room. I see bookshelves around the room that aren't overflowing, I see another filing cabinet in place of the multiple piles that adorn my present office. I see a real storage cabinet. I picture myself warm and cozy, free from the drafts at my feet that are so common in our 200-year-old house. In this fantasy, my feet are propped up as I lean back and gaze out the window—as if suddenly I'll have lots of leisure time. . . . I watch chickadees at the feeder or perhaps a deer browsing by the edge of the orchard on an early mist-filled morning.

How nice it will be to move my desk, books, files, and sundry pieces of electronic equipment out of the southwest bedroom that I've slowly outgrown over the past four years. Even if I still had enough space in my present office—and I don't, as my files and equipment have already crept, like an advancing lava flow, into our living room—I would need to move out. With a newly arrived second daughter, my wife and I need to reclaim our home. Yes, this will be a wonderful new space and even more satisfying to me because of the role it can play in demonstrating how to build with low impact on the environment.

"Look at me, Daddy," Lillian calls. My eyes focus again, my mind blinks back to the present from its distant wandering. Inspired by pushing her bulldozer and giant zucchinis down the steep bank, Lillian has gotten directly involved, turning the steepest portion of the bank into a sort of sliding board. We've long since given up trying to persuade her not to get her clothes so dirty. Let her learn to love the outdoors unencumbered by too many restraints.

We take a walk, Lillian and I, up the hill in back of the house. The pace is slow as she stops to pick stems of grass for her mom. I'm careful not to rush her. Let her poke along and explore at her own pace. Try to delay, for a few more minutes, the inevitable "Daddy, pick me up."

We wind our way up to the upper garden, planted to cover crops for the second year running. Before our family expanded, Jerelyn and I dabbled in organic market gardening. We raised cherry tomatoes, summer squash, cucumbers, and a few other vegetables for a local restaurant, plus several crops for ourselves that wouldn't fit in the small garden by the house—corn and winter squash mostly. Good work. Hard, satisfying work. I plan to cultivate that garden again—maybe next year—and perhaps even expand into the nearby field I cleared of trees the year before last. Maybe I'll plant those strawberries I've been wanting for so long. I really do need to make time for gardening again. Working with the land—maintaining a bond with the earth—gives more meaning to my writing and provides that needed balance to my life-style.

Now with Lillian on my shoulders, we turn into the woods to begin our loop back to the house. We pass the single chestnut tree that struggles each year to get a little bigger before it will ultimately succumb to the chestnut blight. How different these woods must have been when the chestnut was one of the dominant species. We wander down along the decaying row of ancient maples that once separated one sheep pasture from another or perhaps stood along a town road—I've never been able to find out with any certainty which it was. Each year a large section of one of those mammoth sentries crashes to the ground, heard only by the creatures of the forest. The great rotted sections of trunk on the ground are riddled with holes where woodpeckers foraged happily for grubs.

In a few years Lillian will be using the hollow trunks of these maples as secret hiding places with her friends. I vaguely remember some hollow-tree hiding places from when I was not too much older than Lillian. They are good memories. For how many more generations of adventuring children will these particular trees remain, I wonder? And what will these woods look like once the giants are gone, with only the old stone walls marking where they had been? Or will all this woodland be gone by then, replaced by scenic second-home condominiums?

We pass the site that I've often thought would be ideal as a little writer's cabin. Good exposure for solar heating. A majestic view out over the field and down the West River valley below. I picture myself typing away with an eye on the keyboard and an eye out the window watching for a wild turkey or deer.

Fortunately for my career, I think, I decided to put my new office space down by the house, where the cables of modern technology can connect me to the outside world and my livelihood. Someday, maybe, I'll still build the little cabin retreat up the hill. By then I'll be able to power it with photovoltaics. And, who knows, maybe satellite-direct cellular phone technology will obviate the need for phone lines. For now, I'm glad to have put the building right where it is, next to our house.

The new office comes into view as we walk the last stretch back to the house. It looks good from up here. It fits in well with its 200-year-old neighbor. I'm tempted to spend a few minutes nailing up sheathing, but the day is slipping by. I have an article to get into the mail by five. Lillian returns to her sandbank. I return to my office.

Sacred Harp

Tom Slayton

The Strafford Town House, spare and white, lifts its bell tower over the tidy Strafford village green, a chaste symbol of the fierce idealism that carved New England out of the wilderness and that has stamped its character in ways still recognizable. As I get out of my car I can hear singing coming out of the building. Even from where I am, 100 yards away, the stark old melodies and minor chords lofted by more than 200 voices sound clearly, enriching the thin sunlight of early fall. I walk toward the old community meetinghouse.

This is what I have come for. The annual New England Sacred Harp conference is under way and in full voice. The Town House, one of Vermont's most beautiful and famous buildings, was built in 1779, twelve years before Vermont became a state. It's more than likely some of the songs being sung there today were sung 200 years ago, when the Town House was a tiny oasis of hope and order set against a vast backdrop of savage wilderness. Today, the building's moveable pews have been formed into a large square facing the center of the hall, and each section of the large impromptu chorus that has gathered—sopranos, altos, tenors, and basses—occupies one side of the square.

The building itself is the reason I could hear the singing so clearly outside. Just as a guitar box amplifies a vibrating string, so the old wood-frame building picks up the singers' voices and casts them easily across the Strafford green. Feet tap in rhythmic accord, 200 voices raise in unison the stern, old, apocalyptic words, and the floor joists of the Town House can be felt vibrating gravely, rumbling along in time.

What wondrous love is this!
Oh my soul! Oh my soul!
What wondrous love is this,
Oh my soul!
What wondrous love is this,
That caused the Lord of bliss
To bear the dreadful curse
For my soul, for my soul!
To bear the dreadful curse
For my soul!

The sound that fills the building and spills out its open front door is extraordinary; it is like a vigorous cross between American folk music and Renaissance choral music: vivid, soaring melodies, both major and minor (and sometimes, with elements of both), are carried on stark, open chords. The songs use frequent discords, unusual scales and modes, and tricky, exhilarating rhythms, and though they are short—most last no more than five or ten minutes—they are undeniably powerful. They are angular, roughshod, and exciting. When sung by a large group, they are as powerful as a Russian folk chorus and have much of the same quality and feeling. Virtually everyone who writes about these songs agrees they seem quintessentially American because of their vigor, rough harmonies, and general lack of polish. They are now recognized as the oldest composed music in America, and they flourished here in Vermont, very likely in this particular church, two centuries ago.

But they are more than just history. Each song has a rugged beauty all its own, and they are fun to sing. I slip into the back row of the bass section and find my place in *The Original Sacred Harp*, the major existing collection of these tunes. Not every Sacred Harp song is a New England tune. Most, in fact, were composed in other parts of the country, after the tradition had spread there and had begun to die out in New England. Even after the older folk-hymn tradition was replaced in New England by tamer, more conventional-sounding hymns closer to European musical styles, the shape-note songs persisted in the rural South, where the music survives as a living tradition. (The songs are often referred to as "shape-note" songs because of the unusual system of musical notation used to write them down—notes are "shaped" into triangles, squares, and circles to represent the fa-so-la notes of the diatonic scale.)

In the late 1700s and early 1800s in Vermont, traveling music teachers called "singing-masters" wrote many of the best songs and used them as teaching tools. Justin Morgan, better known as the owner of the first Morgan horse, was an early "tunesmith," or composer, of these songs. He and other singing-masters traveled throughout the rough frontier composing and teaching music.

Now, in an age when popular music is a multi-million-dollar industry, and music in a hundred different forms and styles assaults the ear throughout the day, shape-note songs are no longer widely known. But the resurgence of this striking, unconventional handmade music is surprising evidence that the past can sometimes be reborn. And the Strafford Town House on a clear and beautiful fall day is among the best places to go to listen to it.

> *How tedious and tasteless the hours,*
> *When Jesus no longer I see!*
> *Sweet prospects, sweet birds and sweet flowers*
> *Have lost all their sweetness to me.*
> *The midsummer sun shines but dim,*
> *The fields strive in vain to look gay;*
> *But when I am happy in him,*
> *December's as pleasant as May.''*

The singing fills the church, rich and rhythmic. Although not gifted with a strong or beautiful voice, I am soon lost in the music, totally absorbed; I feel like one small member of the heavenly choir and know that if heaven were to be anything like this, I would gladly move in tomorrow.

I first heard this music in college and liked it immediately; it took me roughly fifteen years to work up my courage to attend a local sing, but the music is not difficult and I now go regularly to monthly sings near my Montpelier home and annual sings around the state. I love singing these choral pieces because they are a part of Vermont's history, because they are beautiful, and because singing with a group is, as anyone who has done it knows, a lot of fun.

More than thirty of the singers at this Strafford sing are not from New England at all but from the Deep South—Alabama, Georgia, and Florida. The southerners are regarded by the northern singers as a treasure and have been eagerly welcomed to the sings for several years. Perhaps the Civil War really is over at last.

However, the first meetings between North and South were not without tension. There are some very real, very obvious social and cultural differences between the two groups. The southerners are, by and large, from mainstream, middle-class America, and they dress up for the sings in dresses, suits, and ties. Most of them are older and more conservative than the northerners, who come to sings dressed informally, often in jeans and T-shirts. And there is the touchy matter of religion. These are, after all, deeply religious songs taken from a very specific, quite conservative brand of Calvinist Protestant Christianity. Most of the southerners believe in the literal truth of the texts, which are often derived directly from important doctrinal biblical passages. The northerners, though many of them love the music deeply and respond instinctively to the power and beauty of the texts, are not Calvinists nor even Baptists. They are mostly liberal-to-radical, college-educated music lovers, many of whom were attracted to shape-noting through the folk revival of the 1960s. Elka Schumann of Glover, founder with her husband, Peter, of the well-known Bread & Puppet Theatre, and an avid singer of the music herself, noted wittily in a recent newspaper article she wrote on the resurgence of interest in shape-note singing in Vermont: "The poignant, contrapuntal melodies, stark dissonances, and soul-stirring words seem to have a special appeal for agnostic intellectuals, white-collar professionals, and organic farmers."

As a white-collar Vermont journalist, I can only agree. I don't think I'm more emotional than most people, but I have found my heart lightened by an hour or a day of singing shape-note tunes. And I would be lying if I didn't admit that the old stern words promising salvation, damnation, eternal bliss, or agonies of judgment have brought an occasional tear to my eyes. And I do not think that I'm alone in that. The point is that on some level, the old hymns stir the hearts of people who are religious in a conventional churchgoing sense and people who are not.

The cultural differences between North and South, now apparently resolved by music and friendship and the passage of time, took some overcoming in the early years of the revival. Leonard Spencer of Cabot recalled that at one early North-South sing held in the Haybarn Theatre of Goddard College in Plainfield, one of the southerners pointed out that there had been no opening prayer and that perhaps one should be offered. One of the northerners objected, saying some of those in attendance might be offended by such a prayer.

"Well, no one said anything and the matter was passed over," Spencer said. "But the next year, the southerners didn't come back."

The northern singers quickly realized that a significant social error had been committed, and their leaders quietly let the southerners know that if only they would come back to the New England sings, there would certainly be no further objection to prayer. Opening and closing prayers, often quite fervent, are now offered at each annual New England sing.

Over the years, those differences in style and approach have become less important than the genuine friendship that has developed among the singers, no matter where they come from. Such is the magical power of music that all the superficial elements of appearance and belief are easily put aside, and today, northerner and southerner sing the same words from the same plain hymnal, toes tapping, arms swinging in unison to mark the time, smiles of an extraordinary happiness on many faces as the great, vivid, soaring melodies lift into the wooden church and set it quivering to its very foundation.

> *Hark! The Redeemer from on high*
> *Sweetly invites his fav'rites nigh,*
> *From caves of darkness and of doubt,*
> *He gently speaks and calls us out.*
> *Come, my beloved, haste away!*
> *Cut short the hour of thy delay;*
> *Fly like a youthful hart or roe,*
> *Over the hills, where spices grow.*

Sacred Harp   **95**

Singmaster Larry Gordon notes that much of the music was probably written predominantly for teenagers. "That's who was at the singing schools, basically," he said. "This music appealed to them, and still appeals to them."

It's true. Singing under Gordon's direction with a small chorus in Hardwick one recent summer, the strength of this early Vermont-made music and the effect it can still generate in contemporary Vermonters was obvious to me. Many in that small chorus were high school students, veterans of music classes Gordon was teaching at Hazen Union High School. They were an exuberant, pleasantly unruly, essentially happy bunch, as much a part of the modern world as small-town young people anywhere, complete with blue jeans, punk jewelry, boom boxes, and other items of mass culture. During breaks in practice, they would swing from tree branches outside the church where we practiced, flirt with one another, listen to rock music on their tape decks — and then troop back into the church, sit down with us older folks, and tear into the old tunes with real fervor and enthusiasm. Our practice sessions lasted until nine at night and probably could have gone on longer. They were real fun, partly because of the diverse group that attended (I had forgotten how much fun high school kids can be) but primarily because of the music. I have described it to friends as "200-year-old evangelical rock and roll." It often stands what is left of my hair on end.

We usually ended our practice sessions with "New Jerusalem" by Vermont composer Jeremiah Ingalls. That particular song was a favorite of the Hardwick group, as it is of most Vermont shape-noters, because of its vigorous tempo; clear, multi-stranded polyphonic interplay; and firm, triumphant closure — a musical climax perfectly matched by the Judgment Day triumph expressed in the words of the song:

> *Lo, what a glorious sight appears*
> *To our believing eyes;*
> *The earth and seas are passed away*
> *And the old rolling skies.*
> *From the third heaven where God resides,*
> *That holy, happy place,*

The New Jerusalem comes down,
Adorned with shining grace.

We were not an especially religious group, at least in conventional terms, but that did nothing to lessen the impact of the old hymns. Something definite and undeniable happens when those fiercely uncompromising words are sung to their equally uncompromising tunes. People often asked to sing "New Jerusalem," or some other favorite, over again, and once, when one of the high school kids quipped, "let's just keep singing it all night," I was ready to second the suggestion. No matter how tired I might have been driving up to Hardwick after a day of work, after each sing I always felt refreshed, animated, and full of energy. The twenty-five-mile drive was always shorter going home.

Revitalization—recreation that really re-creates an individual— is what any successful participatory art does for its practitioners, of course. Shape-noting has always been a participatory tradition, and in some ways musically, it's closer to medieval and Renaissance music than to conventional nineteenth-century European-style music. The songs are often based on folk tunes, and the melodic and contrapuntal qualities of the individual lines are more important than their overall harmony, for instance.

Nowadays of course, the words sometimes take on a different meaning than they originally had. For example, there's a direct link between the fear of Judgment Day expressed in many of the old songs and another, more contemporary fear. Composer Jeremiah Ingalls's "Harvest Hymn" uses a grain harvest as a metaphor for Judgment Day—when traditional Christians believed this world would end in smoke and fire.

The fields are all white, the harvest is near;
The reapers all with their sharp sickles appear,
To reap down their wheat, and gather in barns,
While wild plants of nature are left for to burn.
Come then, O my soul, and think on that day
When all things in nature shall cease and decay;
The trumpet shall sound, the angels appear
To reap down the earth, both the wheat and the tare.

Sacred Harp   **97**

Twill all be in vain, the mountains must flee,
The rocks fly like hailstones and shall no more be;
The earth it will shake, the seas shall retire,
And this solid world will then all be on fire.

The idea of the last day, when the world was supposed to be destroyed, fascinated—even obsessed—nineteenth-century Christians. The notion crops up again and again in folk and fine art alike in the 1800s. And though the idea of a day of judgment certainly has less currency now, the suggestion that the world could end in a blast of fire surely carries some weight in this, the nuclear age. The stirring imagery of slippery rocks, fiery billows, and a world on fire can pierce just as deeply into a singer's thoughts today as they could 200 years ago, even though the context is different. The minor tunes of the apocalyptic songs (they're almost always minor, with harmonies as dense and dark as an overcast sky in January) emphasize and add to the catyclysmic, doom-ridden atmosphere.

Another gentler idea is as close to the Vermont soul today as it was 150 years ago, when Ingalls wrote the beautiful song, "Honor to the Hills." He clearly expresses a native Vermont pantheism:

Through all this world below, God we see all around.
Search hills and vallies through; there He's found.
In growing fields of corn,
The lily and the thorn,
The pleasant and forlorn
All declare, God is there;
In meadows dressed in green, there he's seen.

The love of nature and the outdoor world is one of the touchstones of the Vermont character today, as it has been down through the years. The reasons are obvious: Vermonters have long had to accommodate their lives to nature, primarily because there's a lot of it around. A rugged topography, a harsh climate, and a shortage of gold, oil—even decent topsoil—have guaranteed our respect for nature. The well-known beauty of the Green Mountain state has added a touch of reverence to that respect. Whether it's the farmer haying with one eye on the ever-fickle sky or the runner slogging through muck and snow, most Vermonters hunger for, respect, and to some degree stand in awe of the natural world.

Of course, many modern singers do connect with Christian theology when they sing, and it enriches the songs for them. But for many others, there are different attractions, attractions that shape-note music shares with much of the rest of folk art. People who like folk art are attracted to it for a variety of reasons, not all of them purely matters of aesthetics. Many people like such art, for example, because of its undeniable nostalgic pull. It makes us think of bygone times, when life (we like to believe) was simpler. I have to admit there's something of that kind of pleasure involved in my love for shape-note music: I like to think of my Vermont ancestors singing these tunes; I like the notion that the sounds I hear and help make were heard and made by Vermonters who lived in these hills before me.

But there's a deeper attraction than that. Not all folk art, but certainly the best of it, digs deep into the human consciousness and probes the inner workings of our subconscious mind. Whether it's a song about a deceitful man stabbing Pretty Polly to death, a "Jack" tale, a Tree of Life quilt, or a stern, simple Shaker ladder-back chair hung on a bare wall, folk art succeeds most convincingly when it deals in archetypes. We all carry these deep, basic, primeval ideas within us, somewhere back in the dark recesses of our alligator brains: the hero's struggle, the tragedy of the weak, the sanctity of home, the power of detachment, the cycle of life, death, and resurrection. As anthropologists and psychologists have known for years, mental archetypes occur and reoccur with remarkable similarity throughout the tales, songs, and art of the world. They are part of our common human heritage and part of the eternal appeal of folk art.

So, when we contemporary singers belt out "Hampton" by Eliakim Doolittle (another early Vermont composer), we sing and are cheered by the following words:

> *Ye flow'ry plains proclaim his skill;*
> *Vallies lie low before his eye.*
> *And let his praise from ev'ry hill*
> *Rise tuneful to the neighboring sky.*

Sacred Harp   99

God's praise—whatever name we give or don't give Him (or Her)—is certainly being offered at such moments. And that basic, deep-seated human desire to give thanks and to praise the deep, unknown power that invests the earth and makes it good and beautiful finds voice in our song.

We simply don't have, these days, that many opportunities to sing praise, to sing about eternal woe, about joy that never ends, visions so divine, morning flowers cut down and withered in an hour, earth as a humble footstool, old rolling skies, and the New Jerusalem, adorned with shining grace. In our modern rational approach to life, we have impoverished our language and our minds. The deeply religious symbolism of shape-note songs gives us the opportunity to enrich ourselves again. They allow us to sing about the real issues of the heart—life, death, grace, salvation, sin, and resurrection.

I know that I need such times, and I suspect others do, also. Who can say? Perhaps the words we sing, as much as the music itself, help to refresh us. The musical pleasure of singing, the delight in joining in song with others, is surely also a part of the attraction this music gives today. At a really big sing, where people are sure of the music and know lots of different songs, then the stops are pulled way out, people sing enthusiastically, and you find yourself refreshed and renewed in ways you can't adequately express.

This is what history—real history, that takes root in your life—can be: an understanding of the past and a practical use of it to enrich the present and make it fully meaningful. Only a fool would say that living in Vermont, for all its delights, is always easy. One of my own hardest times, I've found, is the butt end of winter: those dreary days in late February and early March when landscapes, sky, work, food, and life itself all seem gray and usually fairly grim. It's just about that time of year, perhaps a week or two beyond then, that the annual Vermont statewide Sacred Harp singing takes place. It always helps.

There usually comes a time in that sing when I can feel the dead weight of winter break and fall away from me. I can't say whether it's the words, the music, the nostalgia, the history, the poetic symbolism, the sense of continuity with my forebears, or the simple joy of singing that brings me out of the dead white past and into new life. But I do know that it happens and quite often is helped along by the singing of William Billings's "Easter Anthem," a song of happiness and triumph that we traditionally sing standing:

> *The Lord is ris'n indeed! Hallelujah!*
> *The Lord is ris'n indeed! Hallelujah!*
> *Now is Christ risen from the dead,*
> *We sing, declaring joyfully later in the song:*
> *Then I rose; then I rose!*

Soprano and tenor parts ricochet back and forth, answering first basses, then altos, then one another. In some passages, all the choirs sing in cheerful unison. The words, notes, rhythms of the piece build in excitement as it continues. It's no wonder that by the end of the song, there's electricity in the air, and we sing, triumphantly and loud, the closing words, meaning them:

> *Thine's all the glory, man's the boundless bliss!*
> *Thine's all the glory, man's the boundless bliss!*

After that, spring itself—even a Vermont spring—can be almost anticlimactic.

A Cabinet of Curiosities

Joseph A. Citro

In 1955, water from nowhere collected on the concave seat of a wooden chair in a Windsor home. Several quarts a day!

In 1977, a monster poked its ugly reptilian head through the calm surface of a bay in Lake Champlain and scared Sandra Mansi half to death. Luckily, she wasn't too frightened to take its picture.

Between 1945 and 1950, seven people vanished without a trace in a "Devil's Triangle" area on Glastonbury Mountain near Bennington. Some—we can be sure—did not simply lose their way. They knew the land, had hunted and fished it all their lives. So where did they go?

Starting in 1886, Dr. Jekyll and Mr. Hyde—or someone very like him—lived in Chester. In 1902 he was arrested. Some say he died in prison, others say he came back from the dead. To this day, no one knows for sure.

In 1759, Major Robert Rogers and his Rangers were challenged by a *wejek* near Missisquoi Bay. In 1985, a West Rutland family was attacked by something very similar. They called it a Bigfoot.

In June of 1838, John P. Weeks of North Danville died and toured Heaven and Hell with two angels as guides. Then, miraculously, he came back to tell the tale. And in the early 1960s, a girl was kidnapped from a camp near Milton and taken aboard a flying saucer. It was only through hypnosis that she could remember the details.

These are all tales of Vermonters and—as artist and humorist Francis Colburn once said—the odd state they are in.

Odd indeed.

In 1970, *Vermont Life* magazine collected thirteen similarly weird tales in a volume called *Mischief in the Mountains*. Though it only scratched the surface of our Green Mountain mysteries, it sells well to this day. Clearly Vermonters and would-be Vermonters have a taste for the bizarre.

Vermont-born myself, I have courted the strange for at least thirty years. In my honorary post as Vermont's Only Horror Novelist, I have collected enough weird-but-true tales to keep new books coming for the next decade. And with the spillover, I can easily fill several *Mischief*-size booklets with Vermont curiosities.

People often ask, why do you write that kind of stuff?

The answer is simple: because they're great stories; they've outlasted any best-seller you can name.

In the 1870s, William and Horatio Eddy conducted materialization séances at their Chittenden farmhouse. Dozens of costumed apparitions would appear in the Eddys' small upstairs room or in a nearby cave. The apparitions were so vivid and stunning that people came from all over the world to witness them. In some circles, Vermont became known as the Spirit Capital of the Universe!

In the early years of this century, impossible torpedo-shaped objects were seen hovering and zooming in the skies above Burlington. The witnesses? None other than Bishop John S. Michaud and former governor Urban Woodbury.

Granted, most people don't see the state exactly the way I do. For some, Vermont is a sort of Yankee Shangri-la, a romantic anachronism of color-changing hills, white postcard villages, and clear blue skies. It's simple and uncluttered, like the seasonal covers of *Vermont Life* magazine.

While the romantics admire white church steeples, I worry about what's hiding in their shadows. While idealists revere our poster-perfect waterways, I wonder about the unknown critters swimming just below the surface. While sweating utopians hike and explore our bountifully forested state parks, I fret about the alien animals lurking just beyond the tree line.

Shadows. Things unseen. Wonders not yet defined or catalogued. This is what I call Vermont's dark side.

A Cabinet of Curiosities 103

Of course, I can never be sure whose perception is more accurate. I admit both are equally romantic. I like to think they're symbiotic, at least for the purposes of my books. Perhaps the clearest vision encompasses both.

In 1971, Audrey Besse, her mother, and a friend saw a long dark spotted creature with two or three humps swimming in a Vermont lake. Another Champ sighting? Not this time, unless Champ moved to Lake Willoughby.

A different Vermont lake: Occasionally someone spots a nine- to twelve-foot half-submerged form lying in quiet water. The creature is described as having a scaled body and a weblike tail. There are forklike antennae on its head. This time it's Champ, right? No. It's Woodbury Lake; the creature is known as the Woodbury Water Witch. Other monsters have been spotted in Lake Memphremagog, the Connecticut River, Dead Creek, and the Winooski....

With monsters in our waters, unidentified objects in our skies, and shambling hairy man-beasts in our forests, perhaps we should not become too complacent in our thinking. In fact, one might be tempted to look around fearfully and conclude that what we call reality is a flimsy facade indeed.

The same crusty old can't-get-there-from-here Vermonter with his legendary reserve, abundant common sense, and smoldering corncob will be quick to tell you that his water supply resulted from the work of a dowser or that there's something kinda peculiar about that abandoned house just down this side of the quarry.

Part of Vermont's mystique is its mystery.

In East Richford there is an antigravity spot not far from the Jay Road. A parked two-ton car left in neutral will begin to move and attain speeds of fifteen miles per hour going uphill!

A cemetery in Middlebury. Check out the grave between Charlotte Moody and Caroline Mead. Buried there are the ashes of a man who died in 1883 B.C. At least that's what the grave marker says. Is it a slip of the stonecutter's chisel? Absolutely not!

One Halloween night a local youth and his high school buddies were carousing in a cemetery near Northfield. They'd had a few beers but swear they weren't drunk. A statue of the Madonna, as if in disapproval, turned slowly and stared at them.

Why do I do it?

It's in my blood, I guess.

My grandfather came here to work on the railroad. I remember him vaguely. He'd sit in his armchair near the kerosene heater, feet propped on an ottoman, and smoke his churchwarden pipe. He was stereotypically down-to-earth, a man of few words, but when he spoke it was often about deaths and suicides and the strange things he had seen when he walked the tracks with his lantern.

My father was more of a storyteller. When I was small he told me how lightning had chased him around the house, how he had watched deer flock to an orchard and grow intoxicated as they munched fallen apples, and how he had seen an enigmatic wispy shape, maybe a ghost, that had floated silently downhill, a few feet above the ground, and the trees had parted to let it pass....

Before Dad died I had learned that ball lightning exists and that it behaves strangely — much as he'd described. Perhaps — who can say now? — it did chase him around the house. I learned that deer *do* become tipsy by feeding on fermenting apples. But it is the third story that makes me wonder — could it be true? Did it happen?

In 1983, farmers at the Ranney Farm in Dummerston discovered twenty-five dead cows in a heap in the center of the barn. The animals were arranged in a perfect circle with feed still in their mouths. All the other livestock nearby were alive and well. There was no evidence of a lightning strike and no other theories to explain what might have happened.

In 1982, Aubre Brogden of Bakersfield was driving home about nine o'clock at night under a full moon. She saw "a large white light moving slowly in the sky." She recalls, "At first, I thought it was a plane about to land, so I flashed my car headlights to warn it off the road.

"And then it started coming toward me!"

Where do these stories come from? Why do they stay around?

Folklorist Richard M. Dorson discusses our New England ancestors: "...lacking books, loving horrors, bred in demonology, and surrounded by dread animals and savages, colonial Americans turned naturally into vivid spinners and eager consumers of folk-yarn. Cradled and nurtured in the wonder-laden atmosphere of a new world and stimulated by a brimstone theology that clothed evil in human form, this native flair for storytelling found continuous expression and ready opportunity with the nation's growth."

Picture this: three ten-year-olds camping out in the backyard. A hundred feet of summer night separates them from the house. The hotdogs are gone, the marshmallow bag is empty. The ice has melted, leaving the Kool-Aid watery but okay to drink.

It's dark, clouds cover the moon. The house lights go out; the parents are in bed.

The white island of light from the Coleman lantern pushes shadows back into the dense woods surrounding the property.

Now, try to tell those boys there is no severed hand clenching and unclenching with infinite impatience just beyond the lantern light. Convince them that one of the dark thick-trunked trees will not pull itself out of the ground and spider along on its roots, looking for a midnight snack.

Or go back even further. You're in an eighteenth-century farm-house. Its nearest neighbor is three miles down the snow-covered, unlit road. Candles flicker. Logs burn in the fireplace. Shadows dance. Imagine a moonless night. Forests and hills crowd the dark drafty dwelling. Now imagine a noise in the attic....

Or loggers. They're camping in the Northeast Kingdom before it was the Northeast Kingdom. Stories again. They talk of the men they've lost to the river. Or the storekeeper who went haywire, killed his wife, then spanked his kids for crying before putting them to bed. The loggers, eyes on the dying camp fire, let their discussion end with a sagely, "Who can say...?"

And the wind howls.

Or is it the wind?

Roberge whispers something about the *windigo*; McNaughton recalls the banshee but keeps his silence.

Recently a Middlebury office building was undergoing renovations. Pounding and power saws must have upset its unseen residents. Silverware flew through the air, shelves ripped from the walls—all sorts of outlandish phenomena happened in front of witnesses. A professional ghostbuster had to be called in so things could return to business as usual.

On one of the Lake Champlain islands there is a house well known to be haunted. Sleeping in one particular bedroom almost guarantees you'll be awakened with the sound of screams ringing in your ears and the sensation of icy hands around your neck.

The thing about myths is that they often turn into facts. So what if that light in the sky is nothing but Venus? Who cares if that specter among the trees is just a wind-driven sheet escaping some neighbor's clothesline? Sure. Fine. We knew it all the time.

But the change can go the other way. Fact, on occasion, can prove to be apocryphal. In school I learned that there were never any real Indians living in Vermont. Today, archeaologists tell a very different story. Native Americans have lived here for 10,000 years! The people Samuel de Champlain spotted in 1609 were native Vermonters, after all.

And—something else I learned in school—that Champlain was the first European to set foot on Vermont soil.

Or was he? Not if you believe a woeful message found on a lead cylinder on the banks of the Missisquoi:

> This is the solme daye I must now die this is
> the 90th day we lef the Ship all have
> Perished and on the Banks of this river I die
> so farewelle may future Posteritye knowe our end.

It is signed by the mysterious "Johne Greye." It's dated November 29, 1564.

Sure, maybe it's a hoax, but what about the fifty-plus stone buildings that have been discovered all around the state? These solid stone igloos have been around longer than anyone can remember, and no one can explain them. One theory is that they were built by seagoing Celts two thousand years before Columbus! Maybe so, maybe not. But the fact remains, no one knows who built them or when or why.

In 1823 the dying Mercie Dale cursed the prosperous Hayden family; they would die out in stark poverty in three generations. Strangely, they did. Just as she'd said. And they left a deserted mansion near Newport that just might be haunted.

Other curses seem to work in Vermont. Especially when articulated by Indians. No one could keep that Brunswick Springs hotel from burning down time after time, just as the old shaman predicted. And a grisly fate awaited Rogers' Rangers as they returned through the Green Mountains with a silver statue stolen from the St. Francis Indians. Perhaps the last thing they heard was an echo of a dying Indian's voice saying, "The great Spirit will scatter darkness in the path of the accursed white men! Hunger walks before and death strikes their trail!"

All the stories in this essay are *real*. They may not be *true*, but that's okay, this is not an essay about truth. If anything, it's about questions. And questions, it might be said, are to the mind what lifeblood is to the vampire. Questions are the catalyst for curiosity, discovery, and, ultimately, creation.

If Edison hadn't asked questions, you might be reading this by candlelight. If Edison hadn't asked questions, he would never have begun working on his communication device—for talking with the spirit world. (He died before completing it, rendering it unnecessary, I suppose.)

Chateaugay, a wild woodland area of steep hills and stark ridges in central Vermont. Moose and large cats are reported with astonishing regularity. A moose isn't too hard to believe, but Vermont's last big cat, a catamount or panther, was killed in 1891. Wasn't it?

August 1987. A well-known Vermont folksinger and a companion were driving along I-89, near Barre, at about one o'clock in the morning. In the black sky, an object that looked like "an upside-down pyramid," lighted on every corner, paced their car for a while. Then it took off at fantastic speed and vanished. "I know it was something weird," the witness reports. "It was as big as a three-story building!" What could it have been?

Sometimes, in rare moments of introspection, I really try to get to the bottom of things. Okay, I ask myself, why? Why do I do it?

Here an honest answer works as well as a lie. See, to me it doesn't matter if the stories are true—that's why I'm a novelist instead of a journalist. What's important is what the stories *do*. And what they do, they do well.

The curiosity they inspire is like our golden link to the fantastic. And fantasy is as nourishing as sunlight.

These wonderful tales are our return ticket to the days of childhood and wonder. They're our bridge to imagination, maybe to creation itself.

They are a magic island in a science-centered world that has no place for goblins and fairies and dragons in the lake.

And the words of the stories are magic words. I have seen them make an old man's eyes sparkle like the eyes of a child. I have seen a whole classroom full of bored high school students sit up and pay rapt attention. And I'll never forget that elderly woman who shook my hand and said, "You know, that reminds me of something that happened when I was a little girl. . . .

The Champlain Islands are dappled with tiny magical castles. Each perfect little structure looks like a fairy tale come to life. Obviously they were created by someone with a strong sense of fantasy.

Or do little castles suggest little people?

In 1894, Sir Arthur Conan Doyle visited Rudyard Kipling in Brattleboro. They discussed the Reverend S. Baring-Gould, who, traveling in a carriage on his way to Montpelier, was besieged by "legions of dwarfs about two feet high running along beside the horses. Some sat laughing on the pole, some were scrambling up the harness to get on the backs of the horses." Had the Reverend Baring-Gould been munching fallen apples?

Okay, so maybe ghosts aren't good for the real estate business. And Bigfoot probably doesn't do much for the Vermont tourist industry. Still, year after year, the stories persist. Perhaps it all goes to show what we have known right along: There is a good deal more to Vermont than meets the eye.

I for one hope it stays that way.

Say, did I tell you the one about the vampire that was killed in Woodstock. . .?

An Outsider's Inside View
of the Legislature

Bill Mares

When I joined the convening Vermont legislature in January 1985, the atmosphere was a heady mix of coronation, wedding, reunion, fish market, freshman orientation, and prizefight.

I arrived a complete novice. I had never run for office before, though my wife had run a plucky race for the House ten years before when we lived in St. Johnsbury. After twenty years as a journalist, describing other people at work, play, mayhem, and creation, I wanted to join the fray. Now, removed to Vermont's metropolis, Burlington, I had scratched the same itch. Had I still lived in Chicago, or New York, or Boston, or even my home state of Texas, I would not have considered such a run. But this was Vermont, where I could ring every doorbell and walk to every house and my campaign expenses would not be more than $1,000. Mostly it took time, twenty hours a week for almost three months, but when it was over, I had won and joined incumbent Representative Mary Evelti in representing the south end of Burlington.

We freshmen had one day in November for "orientation," but that was hardly enough time to savor our victories or to admire the statehouse's marble floors, soaring columns, Civil War banners, and gubernatorial portraits. While the public focused upon the historic inauguration of Madeleine Kunin as the first woman governor of Vermont, we freshmen struggled with the more mundane tasks of learning procedures, how to get bills drafted, where the bathrooms were, and meeting some of our 179 colleagues.

Second in importance to Kunin's elevation was the race for Speaker of the House between Democrat Ralph Wright of Bennington and Republican Robert Kinsey of Craftsbury. I didn't know either of them. Ralph had a reputation as a brass-knuckles politician, and I heard some Republicans talk darkly of what his reign would be like. Conversely, the Democrats dismissed Kinsey as out of step with the changing legislature. The big issue for legislative gossip seemed to be what promises each candidate made to members of the opposite party. Despite a four-seat Republican edge, Wright emerged victorious, giving the Democrats only their second Speaker in the twentieth century.

Once that battle was over, House Clerk Robert Picher administered our oath of office, which read in part, "I. . .do solemnly swear that as a member of this Assembly, I will not propose or assent to any bill, vote or resolution which shall appear to me injurious to the people, nor do not consent to any act or thing which shall have a tendency to lessen or abridge their rights or privileges. . . ."

There followed another small ritual. After returning legislators took their seats, we freshmen drew lots and entered the chamber to claim whichever seats were still free. Randomly, I chose number eighty-two and found myself between Democrat Betty Nuovo, a lawyer from Middlebury, and Republican Roger Kayhart, a Waltham farmer. On my maple flip-up desktop, as on everyone's, were six plastic sets of covers. House Calendars, House Journals, House Bills and a companion Senate set, with accompanying proletarian black shoelaces for adding new pages every day. Inside these covers we would record our work through the session.

Sixty-three House bills greeted us that first day. As I read through them, I didn't know whether to smile or frown. My eyes and mind began to glaze over. These were all serious, I had to assume. But how was I to decide whether to increase the veterans' property tax exemption, or whether to accept DWI samples taken out of state, or whether all drivers should carry liability insurance, or how the state should regulate underground storage tanks?

In the hours and days that followed, we heard the governor speak twice, accepted first readings of bills, and were ourselves assigned to committees. Around the halls and chamber, through the cafeteria moved other legislators with roll call lists hawking their draft legislation to would-be cosponsors. One member advised me to sign up for all the bills I could—that would help for my re-election campaign. I was nonplussed. The reality of my first election had barely sunk in and now I was supposed to be thinking about re-election!

I got my chosen committee, Commerce, and began to meet its members and learn its routines. As I entered the world of utilities, banks, insurance companies, energy regulation, and unemployment compensation, I was still dazed by how much there was to know. I struggled to learn the names and faces of all the members of the two bodies. I tried to read every bill that was submitted. Once we went into our committees, I maintained this compulsion to learn everything as quickly as I could. I volunteered to be clerk because veterans said that lining up witnesses and keeping committee notes was a quick way to learn the system. "By managing the assembly of witnesses, you have a first small taste of power and influence," one member told me.

In the committee, I was relieved to discover that the bills, as introduced, were only the raw materials for our deliberations. They looked fancy, clean, and finished when they arrived on our desks, but in fact they were often the very imperfect translation of legislative draftspeople's understanding of a lawmaker's dream, annoyance, or crusade. It was our job as a committee to decide on the bills' merits, hear testimony, shape them into forms the majority could agree on, and finally take them to the floor to try to convince the entire body of our wisdom and rectitude.

As the weeks went by, I took the measure of my fellow committee members. Only one did I know beforehand, another Burlington representative, Barbara Hockert. The rest were as random a collection as a lifeboat's survivors—among them were a lawyer from Norwich, a hospital administrator from Newport, a retired banker from Derby, a credit union manager from East Montpelier, a retired electrical equipment salesman from Hartford, a political consultant from South Burlington, a small businessman from Chester, and an office equipment company sales manager from Proctor. The chairman, Mike ("Obie") Obuchowski of Rockingham, was only thirty-two but already a seven-term veteran and a former chairman of two other committees. Our home for the next two years was a crowded corner room with a blackboard, a clock, two calendars, and a phone. Our "offices" were our desks in the House chamber, one filing cabinet drawer each, and the table space in front of our seats. I had to share mine with the tape recorder for taking witnesses' testimony. We sat around an oval table that eventually disappeared under the accumulated newspapers, legislative drafts, and special interest reports. Obuchowski's pile grew so tall that by the end of the session, it was dubbed "Mount Obie."

The first bill that came to us was H-5, relating to unemployment compensation. It was sponsored by Representative George Crosby at behest of the *Caledonia Record* newspaper in St. Johnsbury. The bill sought to exclude newspaper stringers or free-lancers from coverage under the unemployment compensation laws. Several newspaper publishers, including one good friend of mine, Chris Braithwaite, owner of *The Chronicle* in Barton, argued the stringers were independent contractors and the unemployment claims of the stringers elsewhere should not be charged against the papers' ratings. The Department of Employment and Training—which administered the Unemployment Compensation system—however, argued they were covered. I was torn between the department's legal interpretation and my respect for Braithwaite. With the majority of the committee I finally voted to table (kill) the bill. (Ironically, six months later, the state Labor Relations Board ruled that the stringers were not employees and therefore the publishers were vindicated.)

In that small debate over newspaper stringers, I saw a similarity and a difference to my career in journalism. As a reporter I was trained to look for both sides to any issue, then lay them out and let the reader decide. Here in politics, I listened to both sides, but then I had to choose one side, even if I agreed with it only 51 percent. To paraphrase Samuel Johnson: "When a politician knows he has to vote in the morning, it concentrates the mind wonderfully." As I learned later, so wonderfully does a roll call concentrate the mind that some people are inclined to "take a walk" when they can't square conscience with constituency.

From the debate on stringers and many more to follow, I gathered a feel for the philosophy of each member around that oval table. Obviously we didn't all think alike. Nor, and this is the important part, were we always consistent with our own voting. That made for the fascinating coalitions and alliances, both in the committee and on the floor. On the big issues, partisanship burred off some independent edges, but as one leader said one day with only a modicum of hyperbole, "on all but the half-dozen issues of pure party, you're free to vote your own way." That didn't mean they wouldn't try to persuade you if they needed the votes, but that was the fascination, the thuggery, and the art of politics.

My first roll call on the House floor was on the hardly earthshaking question of whether to eliminate the six-inch minimum length of trout to be taken in Caledonia and Lamoille counties. All the rest of the counties had gone along with the experts of the Fish and Wildlife Department, who said there would be no harm in letting people take these small trout. The process on the floor was that a member of the Fish and Game Committee "reported" the bill to the rest of the House and then defended the committee's decision. Fish and wildlife bills, I understood quickly, strike some primordial chord in some legislators and almost never fail to arouse even the drowsiest members to fiery parry and thrust. And there was almost always an inverse relationship between the heat of the battle and the effect of the result on most Vermonters.

As a rule I tended to support the biologists in the department—for example, I felt they, not the legislature, should manage the deer herd. But in this case, I thought it was simply not sporting to take trout under six inches, no matter what the biologists said about a high mortality of fish thrown back anyway.

After a few short questions of the bill's reporter, the Speaker rapped everyone into silence and the clerk tolled off the names: "Allendorf of Underhill, Amidon of Bennington, Auld of Middlesex...." As his voice approached the Ms I could see the bill would pass. But, what the hell, I still thought it was wrong, so when the clerk got to "Mares of Burlington?" I said "No!" in a defiant voice. I was both bemused and exhilarated. This was democracy in action, more exciting than when I first voted in 1964. I had voted my conscience, and, I had to admit, it cost me nothing in my district.

My more substantive baptism of fire came on the vote to raise the drinking age to twenty-one. I was torn. How could we allow our kids to vote, make contracts, serve in combat, but not let them drink? On the other hand, I saw merit to the argument that if Vermont was an oasis of legal eighteen-year-old drinking, we could have on our hands the blood of kids from neighboring states with higher drinking ages. To take the pulse of my district, I spent two evenings calling about forty constituents to ask their opinions. They were no help; they were split down the middle. Since one of the most vociferous opponents owned a bar, I said I didn't want to appear to be in his pocket and I finally voted with some unease with the majority to raise the age.

My disquiet didn't end with the vote. My gut warred with my head. These kids were going to drink anyway and probably under more dangerous circumstances than if they did it legally. We were practicing a neo-prohibitionism here and I didn't like it. So the next day, at third (final) reading, on another roll call I reversed my vote. It made no difference to the final outcome, but I felt better nonetheless. One of my constituents, however, was so enraged he vowed he would do everything in his power to unseat me; I heard later that his daughter had been killed by the car of a drunken teenager.

From that vote I learned that in deciding how to vote it is helpful to project myself forward and imagine how I would defend my vote. Maybe that was the paranoid in me, but it did help me in the future.

After a month or so, I realized that I didn't have to read all the bills. When I saw how we gnawed at some bills and never considered others, I learned to be more discriminating in which bills I studied. However, the time I "saved" by not reading all the draft bills now went into the complexities of the bills our committee considered.

Here I discovered how complicated seemingly self-evident proposals could be. Take the case of uninsured motorists. The Commerce Committee received two bills with over sixty cosponsors that required that all drivers to carry liability insurance. At first blush, what could be more sensible public policy than that?

And, indeed, it was good policy. The problem was in the implementation. The process of shaping a bill was like peeling an onion; it got more pungent (and complex) as we proceeded.

As we heard more and more testimony about the experience of other states with draconian mandates, and we learned that their rates of uninsured motorists were higher than Vermont's, we lowered our sights. Finally, we came up with a bill that said one must carry liability insurance, but the lack of it would only be discovered at the time a driver was stopped for some other violation. We thus tried to balance the administrative capacities of the state police and the Department of Motor Vehicles with the citizens' desire to have every driver carry liability insurance.

One of the most exhausting things about that first session was the constant activity and the inextricable interweaving of people and issues. As clerk, I had to scramble around the building lining up sponsors, witnesses, and bureaucrats. But even as a regular representative, I had to exchange greetings or information or jokes with well over 100 individuals a day. A mixture of curiosity and obligation made me feel I should know what everyone else was doing. It made me think of a school principal making the rounds. To all I had to be polite. By the end of the day my face would be frozen into a tired, ironic smile.

Representing Burlington in Montpelier has its special tensions. A hundred years of envy of the Queen City infused the votes of some legislators on any bill that seemed to benefit Burlington. And whenever former Burlington Mayor Bernie Sanders excoriated the legislature as he loved to do, there were plenty of legislators who were delighted to make that long-standing animus personal.

When four Burlington charter changes to increase local taxing powers came up for legislative approval, both sides sharpened their knives. Supporting the changes during the floor debates, I said if we wanted to shoot ourselves in the fiscal foot, as some had suggested, then so be it. That's the essence of local control. My arguments were unpersuasive to those who feared a Balkanization of taxing authorities in the state and especially to those who didn't want Bernie loose in the state's fiscal china shop. The charter changes went down resoundingly.

As the session progressed, I found the going harder, not easier. The more I learned, the more I felt I had to learn. I seemed to be running faster and faster to stay in the same place. When I added to those duties the necessary consultations with constituents, I found myself almost as tightly bound as Gulliver. I got one warning. When the nurses' association came to the statehouse for a day and gave health checks, I found my blood pressure had risen over the danger point. By the end of the session in early May, I had lost ten pounds and I was exhausted.

Two months later, I had a heart attack. The damage turned out to be minor, requiring no surgery, and I was out of the hospital in a week. But it scared me. The doctors were loath to ascribe it to the pressures of the legislature, but in retrospect I am sure my headlong pace and personality were factors. As I lay in an intensive care bed at the Medical Center Hospital of Vermont, I thought back to something my mother had told me. She said I had always taken on the world's woes. Once, when I was three, during World War II and there were some newspaper pictures of civilians killed in Nazi reprisals, I had said, "We can't let them hurt our world." Maybe I was trying to take on too much. And I remembered the sardonic graffiti from college: "Death is nature's way of telling you to slow down."

I didn't want another heart attack, but I didn't want to quit. I loved the mixture of issues and personalities, which was politics. I wanted to go back and serve my constituents, my flock, not just those in my district but all the people of the state. If I went back into the fray, I knew I would have to slow down and follow Reinhold Niebuhr's prayer to know the difference between what I could change and what I couldn't.

I came back the next year determined to pace myself. I gave up my job as clerk. I took short naps at noon instead of gossiping over lunch. With more time to myself, I think I came to understand the system better. I could see how people counted chits to be traded at the appropriate time. As I learned more of the rules, I could see how some people used them to delay, obfuscate, or kill. I understood that warning lights should greet a bill described as "just a little housekeeping bill," such as when a proponent argued for changing the "may" to "shall" in a particular law. I learned that with some people there was an inverse relationship between the number of times they spoke on the floor and his or her influence. I began to learn whom I could trust, who were the

An Outsider's Inside View of the Legislature   117

sycophants, the windbags, who seethed with ambition, who went about their business with silent effectiveness.

Shaping a bill made me feel like a short-order cook serving a café with fifty seats. You try to keep all the dishes straight, but of course they don't cook for the same length of time and they don't go to the same customers, who all want their orders first. Meanwhile, you are not alone in that kitchen, not hardly. You have 179 other cooks (not counting the governor and all the lobbyists) who want to season the dishes a different way, think they ought to be baked, or grilled, or fried, some longer, some shorter. Some of them don't even like the dish and don't want to cook it. And some of them, even if they like the dish, don't know how to cook.

Eventually you get the dishes to the counter. No matter that the customers may not recognize the dish, nor even want it. Your fellow cooks, having served up the meal, say "take or leave it," even if the eggs Benedict are scrambled, the fried chicken is soup, and the steak tartare is a charred burger.

(I remember thinking at the end of one session: Suppose we came up here for two years and passed only a budget; the rest of the time we would spend expurgating obsolete laws, repairing the cracks and frayed edges in still serviceable laws. Wouldn't that be a sterling service to the people of Vermont?)

Such mangling and revisions were inevitable considering the dozens of perspectives, egos, philosophies, constituencies, and competing legislation affecting a particular bill. I never stopped being awed by the sheer range of issues we had to deal with: criminal sentencing guidelines for judges, universal health insurance, bridge financing, the length of trout, putting the state into the retail power business, certifying psychotherapists, and evaluating the true cost of educating a child, to name just a few.

Perhaps in no other field of endeavor is ambition so naked, yet politicians wrap all their acts in the purple raiment of the public good. In few other jobs ought skins to be so thick yet are so thin. In few other activities is there so much artlessness on the surface and so much calculation underneath. We politicians sail along like innocent pleasure craft, but few of our boats lack torpedoes beneath the waterline. I don't think anyone was a complete megalomaniac. Nor was any legislator a complete wimp. Between those extremes on the spectrum of power we found our respective point according to temperament and ambition.

Raw power did not suffice often; civil behavior and good humor were also vital. Schmoozing was integral to good politicking. Most of the people I worked with liked people. They were interested in their fellow legislators, even when they disagreed with them. There were a few misanthropes who were, in turn, roundly disliked. But in the tight tense quarters of the legislature, people needed to be extroverts. If you didn't like people invading your "space," being solicited as baldly as by a streetwalker, if one didn't like being interrupted 50 to 100 times a day, you were probably in the wrong game. I didn't socialize enough, partly because I commuted almost every day, and evenings were the stellar time for relaxing. Also, I think my outsider streak kept me at arm's length. It was through those legislative card games at lunch, the communal newspaper reading over breakfast, the random socializing in the corridors, on the floor, over coffee, or beer, or tobacco that legislators got to know and trust each other, trading stories, information, and, ultimately, favors.

And how people gossiped! It reminded me of high school and the endless fascination of "who was going with whom." During a debate about whether we legislators should get a 30 percent salary increase, one member stridently defended the raise because "we have no benefits." I rose to disagree. "Of course, we have benefits," I said. "Why, this is the only job I've ever had, other than journalism, where I was paid to gossip."

Another advantage of schmoozing is the cultivation of friends who can tell you what's going on. Since you can't be on every committee, you need someone on each whom you can trust. So, when you have only five or ten minutes to learn about a piece of legislation, you are not totally in the dark when the vote comes.

Votes on complex issues were hard enough by themselves. When we added partisanship for its own sake, they became tougher still. I had taken an oath of office to the state of Vermont, not to the Democratic party or its leadership. I wanted to be free to decide when I was right and my party was wrong. Yet, I knew intellectually that unless you had some discipline, a party program would be nigh impossible to pass.

Someone told me once: Even if you agree with the leadership on every bill, you ought to be contrary every once in a while, just to keep them from taking you for granted.

One year the governor pushed a so-called homestead bill, which was supposed to solve the property tax dilemma. I thought the bill was mostly words, and I let it be known I would vote against it. Successively, I was lobbied by the governor, Majority Leader Paul Poirier, Speaker Wright, and Senator Phil Hoff and told this was a vital vote. By the time Hoff got to me, I was bemused by all the attention and unmoved to change my vote.

"Why all this pressure?" I asked Hoff.

"This is not a lot," he said. "If you were known as a waverer, you would have gotten real heat!"

The session of 1987 marked another transition for me. I became vice-chairman of the Commerce Committee. In that year we had three major bills before us — interstate banking, the deregulation of the telephone industry, and a move to put the state into the retail electric power business. All three were controversial in different ways. The most bitter for me was the "power bill." On its face, the issue was the protection of a historical anomaly: a block of cheap power from the New York Power Authority. The Federal Energy Regulatory Commission had been asked to rule whether Vermont qualified as a "public body" and therefore deserved the power. In one piece of legislation in 1985, we had changed the law to make the state the purchaser of the power. But the principal proponents of this bill were hunting far bigger game. They wanted to make the state the direct competitor of the private (and public) power companies.

I saw no reason for the state to sell electric power at retail, especially when it was also regulating the companies with whom it would compete. That struck me as both hypocritical and bad public policy. As a Democrat I was supposed to believe that public power was automatically better, more humane than private power. But if that were the case, why were the municipally owned and cooperative utilities united against this bill?

I finally went along with the bill because I couldn't answer the charge that I might "lose" that block of cheap power. If ever there were a 51-percent vote, it was mine on this bill.

In my third term, given a choice between staying on Commerce and a chance to be chairman, and moving to another committee, I went over to Education. If there was a single reason for this switch, it was my son, Timothy's, entry into the first grade. All the abstractions of education were suddenly transformed into flesh and blood—mine. Rather than having a big role in utilities, banking, and insurance legislation, I preferred a small part in shaping state educational policy, especially in this time of ferment and reform.

Being a "grunt" on the Education Committee also gave me more time to devote to the Statehood Bicentennial Commission. As one of four legislative members, I had become very attached to the celebration of Vermont's 200th birthday. I wanted the celebration to spawn as much interest as possible and for us to create results of enduring merit and value. Since Vermont was the first new state to join the original thirteen, it was particularly important that we do a good job. So I poured myself into a variety of activities, from speaking engagements, to developing bicentennial license plates, to lobbying my fellow legislators for more money.

By the middle of my third term, I began to wonder if I should call it quits. Oh, yes. I enjoyed the heady feeling of being in the know and debating some of the great issues of the day. I liked being part of this legislative construction crew, even though sometimes we built Towers of Babel as well as Taj Mahals. I liked the clubbiness of the place, some of the pomp and circumstance, special license plates, and being addressed as "the honorable." I liked doing small favors for my constituents and my colleagues.

At the same time, some parts of the job were increasingly noisome and wearying. For example, the sessions grew longer and longer. There was more work in the summer and fall. I saw the day coming when I would have to put "politician-writer" on my income tax form, not the reverse. I felt more alienated from the jingoistic brand of partisanship—Republicans who voted with the Democrats were "statesmen," Democrats who voted with the Republicans were "traitors."

I realized, too, that I was probably too thin-skinned for part of this work. I could not separate my private personality from my public one, that public being who was expected to be the lightning rod for lobbyists' guile, constituents' ire, opponents' fire. One result was that in floor debate I was inept, at best. I could give a good prepared speech, but in debate I failed miserably.

Maybe the time had come to go back to the typewriter and give someone else a chance. Yet, I longed to see the bicentennial celebration through to the finish at the end of 1991. Educational reform in Vermont was blossoming, and I had a cockpit seat on the Education Committee. I decided to wait until a month after the end of the session to see how I felt.

On balance I would give myself a C+ for my accomplishments and service. To the experience I would give an A. Since I never expected to win in the first place, I had six years of fascinating work, gratis.

The First Lesson

Fred Stetson

In his more philosophical moments, my father, seated at the head of our dark-mahogany dinner table, liked to launch forth with an evening lecture. I have only vague memories of the contents of these talks. But, to this day, I remain certain he often liked to take the bite out of his monologues by winding up on a bemusing note such as, "Here endeth the first lesson." At other times he closed with, "Do and I say, not as I do."

Over the years, I'm sure I've repeated the latter dictum—or versions thereof. But I never much believed in it. From eighteen years of active and reserve military experience and twenty-two years of watching people as a reporter, I've discovered that true leaders lead by example, not by what they say. Furthermore, what people do, more than what they say, is what establishes or undermines their integrity. That thought remains uppermost in my mind as I reflect back on a summer day when sudden, unexpected blustery winds, gusting up to twenty-three knots, turned a sail on Lake Champlain into a test—a test of a father's leadership and his daughter's trust.

The morning began without any hint of danger. Light rain showers and a gray overcast gave way to gray-white cotton scud, followed by a warm sun breaking down through the scattered clouds. The early-morning showers put a moist, dewlike sparkle on the grass and pines around our summer camp at Starr Farm Beach on the edge of Lake Champlain. About five miles north of downtown Burlington, the "camp" is really a turn-of-the-century, two-story, shingled house with brown-stained shingles and crimson trim. It sits on a thirty-foot cliff overlooking a section of the lake that stretches twelve miles across to New York. From here, you can watch severe weather churn across the water and intensify. In August 1983, a tornado ripped into the Starr Farm area, snapping tall, majestic seventy-year-old pines, shattering glass picture windows, and crushing summer cottages. The vision of that storm, which brought the most hideous, bizarre sky I've ever seen—a cauldron of vacuous, shifting, steaming clouds with a sickly green and white and black color—wasn't on my mind when we planned our sail. At first I thought the rains might stop us, but when the skies cleared, I gathered our gear and headed for the edge of the lake.

I'd looked forward to this morning for a long time. I'd been thinking about a pleasant sail and some time alone with Lizzie, who had just returned from a four-week summer riding camp. Lizzie's one of those eleven-year-olds who is not hard to love. She has a dimpled smile, curly strawberry blond hair, and a beguiling shyness. She may not be the most talkative person in the world, but she has a quick mind and a fast memory. She loves to perform dance routines and favorite songs. One of her very favorites is one of mine, too—a funny tune called, "Welcome to My Fog."

This sail was going to be one of the first tryouts of my latest infatuation, a Laser II sailboat. Though not a new design, this is definitely a high-tech performer. The fiberglass boat has an extremely large sail area for a twelve-footer; the mast stretches through two rooms in our basement, and the sail could drape two or three queen-size beds. In stiff winds, these boats, with flat planing hulls, can easily approach twenty knots. The guy who sold me the boat cautioned that in winds exceeding ten knots, you need two heavy adult males "to hold the thing down."

But on that August day, winds were five knots or less, and morning temperatures were in the high sixties, nudging seventy degrees. Still, I knew that in late August conditions on the lake can change rapidly. The night before, for example, early evening temperatures dropped from sixty-seven down to fifty-nine in less than one hour. Sometimes, on those late summer days, cool Canadian breezes even give a distinct hint of fall. So we pulled warm clothes over our bathing suits and brought extra clothing, dry and protected in a plastic bag, should we need it. After flying army helicopters for more than 3,500 hours, I've become safety conscious, too, so we took the obvious step of wearing life preservers, and I placed a paddle in the shallow cockpit just in case.

About 10:30, after storing our gear and rigging the sails, we pushed off from the rocky shoreline. I headed south, paralleling the jagged cliffs; we had no particular destination in mind. In the far distance across the lake, we could see the green and rock-faced Adirondacks. Being a weekday, there was little activity on the water. In fact, I can remember seeing no other boats.

I took the tiller and asked Lizzie to sit on the upwind rail to help keep the boat flat. But the wind was so slight and unsteady that she had to continually come off the rail to sit in the center of the boat and balance our weight. Still, the skies were largely clear, and only a few puffs of scattered white clouds remained. We felt comfortable and secure.

But in minutes, our sense of security evaporated. A flukey wind ruffled around the sails as though whipped by an unseen eggbeater. The mainsail luffed and snapped. The boat stalled. I tried to head off the wind, to refill the sails with a steady breeze. But, I couldn't find it. The light southerly breeze had turned into a furious windmill.

"We're getting strange winds," I told Lizzie, though I could see from her face she knew that very well.

The sailboat lurched forward then stalled, making fitful jerky jump starts; generating or sustaining steady forward momentum was impossible. Then the wind stiffened directly out of the west and we shot ahead, leaving the lakeshore behind. The boat snapped into a heel and the leeward rail leaned hard into the water, the classic racing picture. Then, just as quickly, the hull flattened and kissed along the surface. I shifted my position—in and out of the cockpit—trying to balance the boat as it gyrated back and forth, behaving like some wild seesaw. I didn't have time to tell Lizzie to do the same. I was too busy, too preoccupied, and too scared to do anything but react. I tried everything I could to hold the thing down, but the boat skimmed on, carrying us farther and farther offshore—almost a mile from our protected harbor and beach.

Finally, I felt brave enough to bring the Laser about in a tack in hopes of heading home. Almost immediately, we heeled hard.

Jesus, I thought, I have no control whatsoever. As fast as possible, I released the main sheet, hoping to dump the wind out of the sail. It didn't work. The hull rotated—about seventy degrees—raising us high in the air, lifting the centerboard clear out of the lake. The downwind rail submerged, sheets of spray splashed through the wire rigging. Then the trailing end of the boom and mainsail dragged in the water, and I knew we were done for.

The roll continued, the hull rotated ninety degrees to the surface, stopped, and began to sink—sideways—straight down.

Lizzie cried and let out a painful, sad murmur—something like, "noo...noo"—something telling of real fear. She turned around and hung onto the rail as the boat slid downward. I faced the same way and cradled her in my left arm as the hull settled. Together, "standing" side by side, we eased into the cool lake, up to our chests. The Laser stopped and lay on her side, the mainsail and jib lolling flat just beneath the wind-whipped surface.

This sucks, I thought. Here I am, introducing my eleven-year-old daughter to Lake Champlain sailing, and we're sinking a mile offshore.

"It's okay, it's okay," I said, trying to calm Lizzie as we let go of the hull, swam through tangled sheets and rigging, and made our way toward the bow.

By the time we reached the other side, the boat rolled some more and stopped, inverted, with sails pointing straight down and centerboard pointing straight up. This is serious, I thought, while trying to stay calm. I'd been here before, though. I'd righted a Laser in rougher winds; I'd sailed through a squall in another small open-cockpit sailboat; and I'd raced sixteen-foot Mercurys off the Massachusetts coast. "It's okay," I kept telling Lizzie, "we'll be all right."

But whether to her my inner conviction matched my outward bravado, I'm not so sure, even to this day. Perhaps I might find the answer if I asked myself why I was so repetitious in this moment of supposed fatherly calm. To be honest, I was worried. The winds continued to increase, doubling, then tripling their original speed of about five knots. Rolling waves rocked the boat. Quickly, the late-August water felt cold. I told Lizzie to crawl up on the inverted hull and catch her breath. She reached for the centerboard, I pushed from behind, and she pulled herself up. After a minute or two, I told her to slide back into the lake so we could attempt to right the boat. As soon as she reached the water, she began to shiver and cry. But, with our life jackets on, I felt safe even though Lake Champlain is about 200 feet deep where we capsized.

Together we reached up, grabbed the centerboard, and pulled. Slowly, the white hull began to rotate and the sails, with broad blue, white, and purple stripes, neared the surface, broke free, and began to rise. For a moment we were elated as the Laser stood tall and straight upright in the correct position. But then we watched in agony as she continued through the roll and capsized again. Wet sails flopped over our heads and fell back into the water.

"It's...not...working," Lizzie wailed.

By this time she was shaking, so we decided, rather than try again, to simply climb back on the inverted boat and sit there, straddling the hull.

"There goes our bag," Lizzie said.

About twenty-five yards downwind, I saw our white plastic bag, filled with sweatshirts, drifting away in the heavy winds and waves. I slipped off the boat, swam to the bag, recovered it, and returned to join Lizzie on the inverted hull. A few minutes later, she noticed our canoe paddle floating away, and after a moment's hesitation, I recovered that, too. Despite all my aviation survival training, which emphasizes staying with your craft, I thought any gear, especially a paddle, would be useful and should be retrieved if at all possible. I also felt I needed to do something, anything, to assuage my growing feeling of guilt at getting Lizzie into this jam.

As we straddled the hull with the bow pointed into the westerly winds, I asked myself again and again—why did I do this? Why did I make such a mess of our first sailboat outing? One of my big fears was of the fear I was instilling in my daughter. Would or could she enjoy sailing again?

Most of the rolling waves felt like a mild buck from a lurching horse. But sometimes the undulating water lifted the hull and threw us off balance. Lizzie clutched the centerboard while I straddled the boat right behind her, grabbing for the board over her shoulders. I tried to keep the bow pointed into the wind, using the paddle to steady our direction.

"What are we going to do?" Lizzie asked.

The First Lesson 127

I did not have a ready answer, exept to say the wind was blowing us ashore and I could paddle as well. Unwittingly, and perhaps subconsciously, I skated a fine line between the need to keep Lizzie's morale up and the need to give her an honest picture of what was happening.

"How long will it take?" she persisted, a good reporter, wanting details.

About two hours, I guessed, after looking at the distant cliffs of Starr Farm. But after several minutes of slow drifting, I could tell she wasn't satisfied with that answer.

"How long will it take?" she asked again.

"We're okay, we're safe, someone will see us," I said, feeling a bit irritated.

But in all directions, I could see only two boats. One was a sailing yacht at least five miles to the north; another was the large Burlington ferry, steaming back and forth far to the south, unresponsive to our plight. When we weren't lurching back and forth, I felt we could withstand a long afternoon on the lake. But Lizzie could not stop shaking. Although temperatures were in the high sixties, the brisk westerlies made the air feel ten to fifteen degrees colder.

I opened our plastic bag and pulled out a dry sweatshirt. With the boat still rolling and bobbing over two- and three-foot swells, Lizzie managed to remove her life jacket and wet shirt, then pull on her soft sweatshirt. She replaced her life jacket, then took off her wet pants, leaving her clad in her bathing suit. We continued to buck back and forth, and once or twice, the swells were strong enough to make us lose our balance and slip backwards.

After about forty-five minutes, we'd made little progress toward shore. But, I told Lizzie, we were safe because the wind and paddling would take us ashore. I didn't tell her it might also take us to the cliffs. But I felt reasonably confident that barring any unforeseen happening, two or three hours of steady paddling and blowing westerlies would take us back to Starr Farm. Our progress was slow, if not invisible, but we remained dry, and, I assured myself, the overturned boat could serve as a life raft for as long as we could stay on top of it.

Still, my uncertainties must have been evident. I kept a kind of stoic countenance, while Lizzie kept a quiet watch. Together, we drifted slowly, backwards, across the lake. After another half hour, I'd given up cheerleading. I groped for something new and encouraging to say. But no sooner had I sunk into a moment of despair, when I looked up and saw a large power boat heading directly toward us. Sheets of water sprayed to either side of the V-shaped hull as the boat plowed through the rolling waves.

"Here comes a boat," I told Lizzie, too relieved to shout.

In minutes, a forty-foot Coast Guard patrol boat slowed seventy-five yards to the southeast of us, then motored toward our stern. Three crewmen in dark blue pants and light blue shirts manned the craft. All wore orange life vests. The patrol boat's heavy aluminum hull eased alongside, falling and rising in the swelling seas. The helmsman inched the boat forward, then back, then forward, then back—each time trying to approach without crushing us.

"Watch your feet!" one of the crewmen yelled.

Christ, that's all we need, I thought, to have the cutter crush our feet with its bashing hull. Fortunately, the crew remained patient, and they eased off to come back at a better angle.

"What are they doing?" Lizzie asked, thinking she was watching some kind of a perverted docking drill.

After several tries, the patrol boat pivoted, so her stern became a nearby platform, about two and a half feet above the water. Quickly, I lifted Lizzie and handed her to the outstretched arms of a crewman who hoisted her aboard. A moment later I followed and the cutter backed away, leaving the inverted bare white hull, for the moment, lolling in the waves. I found Lizzie below decks, huddled in a gray blanket, curled up on a lower bunk facing the inside of the hull, not saying a word. I left her alone.

Up top, I offered to dive back into the water to attempt to right the boat by myself. But the Coast Guardsmen, who stared past me with serious and businesslike looks, seemed little interested.

For the next hour they tried to right the sailboat. One crewman threw a grappling hook over the hull, trying to catch the rail or rigging. They asked nothing of me, which made me feel my nautical advice, or what little I might know about Lasers, was, at this point in time, worth next to nothing. In fact, after finding my services so little in demand, I had the distinct feeling that rescuees might be considered excess baggage on a Coast Guard patrol boat.

As the Coast Guard vessel rose and fell, I feared it might crush or at least crack the fiberglass sailboat. Time after time a crewman threw the grappling hook attached to a chain and rope over the hull. But the hook and chain rattled and slid off and fell limply into the water. Once or twice, the helmsman got the boats too close together, making me wince with every passing wave. I looked down and saw a foot-long orange and black scratch mark, the colors of the Coast Guard, on the Laser's hull. Still, no serious damage was done, and though these efforts were mounting into a long ordeal, I said nothing. Those who require rescuing a mile offshore shouldn't be offering too much advice to their rescuers. And I felt simply grateful to be aboard a ship with the power to overcome the winds and waters of the lake.

After several more unsuccessful tries with the grappling hook, the Coast Guardsmen received a call from their base operations, about five miles south in Burlington. The base radio operator asked for a position and status report. Upon hearing of the fruitless righting attempts in the rough waters, the base guardsman offered to send out a smaller boat, a nineteen-foot fiberglass craft with inflated pontoons on either side. In another twenty minutes, the pontoon boat appeared and drove alongside the wallowing sailboat. While one crewman grabbed the Laser, another reached over with an oar and jammed it into the now-vacant centerboard slot. The oar splintered and broke off into two pieces. The crew members pulled alongside a second time and placed another oar deep into the slot. This time, the oar held. A crewman leaned back, holding the oar like a fulcrum, to right the sailboat just as Lizzie and I had tried to do.

Slowly the Laser turned upright, and the sails broke the surface and flailed back and forth in a tangled mess of lines and wires. The mainsail was too tangled to lower so the Coast Guardsmen lashed it around the mast in a sick-looking nest. Surely, I thought, there's no sailor's indignity worse than seeing the sails, the sole means of motion, wrapped up like a terminal basket case. I could feel Lizzie looking on in disgust. After lashing this mess together and securing other lines and gear, the crewmen lashed the sailboat to the side of the pontoon craft and radioed that they were ready to take the Laser ashore.

Lizzie and I thanked the rescuing crew and stepped onto the pontoon boat, which started toward Starr Farm Beach, a half mile to the east. I held one of the wire stays to help keep the Laser upright in the waves. And, in a move that made me feel useful for the first time since the incident began, I gave the Coast Guardsmen directions to the beach, past a rocky shoal and around a large underwater concrete pier. We reached the rolling shallows off the beach, the crewmen untied the Laser, and Lizzie and I jumped overboard and waded toward the beach alongside the Laser. The sailboat, half filled with water sloshing back and forth in the cockpit, immediately capsized again.

But, in only about four feet of water, there was no problem. I simply held the mast and sails at waist level as the stiff winds pushed the boat ashore. Lizzie scampered ahead and ran home to find warm clothes. A smiling neighbor met me at the beach, and I was relieved that a "what the f——k have you been doing?" look never crossed his face. "Little rough out there," was all he said.

Together we spent several minutes untangling the sails, sheets, lines, and halyards, then hauled the boat onto the dry beach and released a one-inch diameter drain plug in the transom. For several minutes a steady stream of water poured from the hull. Freed of this weight, the Laser was easy to pull ashore and secure.

In retrospect, I think about this day on Lake Champlain with many mixed emotions and questions. What would I have done differently? Why didn't I prepare better for an unexpected wind? Why didn't we practice capsizing in shallow waters? Was my experience or my behavior on the water any worse or better than that of those involved in the 301 other boating incidents requiring Coast Guard assistance that summer? How did I stack up? Were there any details of my incident recorded in the Coast Guard records?

"It was just logged that everything went fine," I was told when I called later.

To be honest, I'm not sure what Lizzie thinks about all this. I saw her fear on the water. I saw her regain control as we rode out the waves on the shaky inverted hull. But I know her first "day-after" thoughts were not the best. "I completely panicked," she told her mom.

Nevertheless, in a couple of days we returned to the lake for another sail under sunny skies and gentle breezes. I think that's a hopeful sign, but I suspect she'll remember standing in the half-inverted, sinking Laser long after she'll remember those sunny skies and gentle breezes.

Nature tests the trust between a father and daughter in unexpected and fleeting ways and can determine whether a father passes the test and makes the grade. And though I feel confident that such trust is built mostly not on one afternoon's sail — or mis-sail — but upon years of love and friendship, months after my adventure with Lizzie, I'm still awaiting the results. And it may be years before I receive them.

Here endeth the first lesson.

They No Longer Play Softball on Main Street

Lennie Britton

The dust clouds from the construction of Interstate 91 hung in the air above Ascutney in the summer of 1964. My grandparents watched the slow-approaching storm from their dairy farm in Hartland twenty miles away. The farm had been staked out by a surveying crew months before, and fluorescent orange ribbons in the cornfield marked the impending path of the highway. The pieces of vinyl looked out of place on the farm, like a tattoo on the arm of a small child. The 200 acres, which had been in my family for generations, stretched out from the Connecticut River toward Mount Ascutney. Aunt Betty was proud of telling people that King George's name was on the deed. My grandfather had set milk production records with his herd of rag-apple Holsteins on this farm, while my grandmother fastidiously tended to the house and gardens. The appearance of a single dandelion on her lawn was not tolerated. She would dispatch the weed as quickly as its yellow head disrupted the green order of her yard. I used to hunt dandelions for her in the spring, gleefully presenting the kill for her inspection.

My grandparents loved their land. It was part of them. Now they faced the specter of a four-lane highway carving through its heart. Eminent domain, the government lawyers told them; Vermont had to be accessible to the rest of the world. That summer, my family would huddle together trying to figure out a way to stop the unstoppable. From time to time, the air was punctuated with the dull report of blasting from down the valley as the construction crews struggled against the great veins of ledge in their way. I could see as the dust clouds got closer the worried look in my grandparents' eyes changed to desperation, and so my unease also grew. I was only nine years old, but I understood that what was about to happen would not only ruin our farm but forever change our family. The farm was the center of our lives, where we all came together as one. Once it was gone, there would be no replacing that safe haven. No more midday suppers where the adults talked politics and the day's business. No more family Christmases in the big room on the south side of the house.

One day that summer my grandfather got a phone call that made him quiet. He put down the receiver and asked me to take a ride with him. We drove in silence to Ascutney. Off in the distance I could see smoke in the sky. As we got closer to the smoke, I could see cars and pickup trucks pulled over where a stand of old sugar maples met the road. My grandfather stopped the car and we got out. Nearby, several men were standing in silence around a smouldering cellar hole. One of the men said something to my grandfather. I looked at the heavy construction equipment poised beyond the cellar hole, then at the singed cows scattered in the field across the road. The air smelled like a barbecue. Two dogs roamed about, moving from person to person, sniffing for their master.

The farm belonged to Romaine Tenny, who had lived there all his life. He had fought the interstate and, for a short while, had halted the construction. But the day before, the sheriff had ordered him off his farm. My grandfather moved to me and told me Mr. Tenny had burned himself down with his house. We joined the other men and stared into the blackened cellar hole, the embers still producing heat. I was suddenly filled with panic. What if my grandparents did the same thing when the bulldozers arrived at the farm? I rode home full of dread, trying to make sense of what I had seen.

Several months after Mr. Tenny burned himself up in his home, I watched from the screened-in back porch of my grandparents' farmhouse as the same construction equipment I saw at the Tenny farm arrived in our cornfield. I watched my grandparents closely as they tried to ignore the giant machines—pretend they didn't exist. They flattened the corn and hay fields and made the dishes clatter angrily in the kitchen as they thundered clumsily past the farmhouse. A carpet of dust settled on the lawn. Soon the knoll where my grandfather had taught me how to call the cows in for milking was gone, the earth moved to make an on ramp for the new highway. Then the blacktop appeared, spewing out of the back of slow-moving machines, frantically attended by a crew of tar-covered men.

My grandparents stoically tried to make the best of what was happening to them. They tried to carry on with life. But 1964 was the last year corn was planted on our farm in Hartland. While the heavy equipment stampeded freely around the farm, my grandmother's health failed. She died the following year, her heart broken. With his wife gone and his farm dissected, my grandfather also quickly lost his will to live and was dead by the time the highway had reached White River Junction. His funeral in the big room on the south side of the farmhouse was the last time all my family was together.

Not long after the interstate crept its way off toward St. Johnsbury, the first newcomers arrived in my homeroom at school in Woodstock. These were kids I hadn't known in Boy Scouts or Little League or Sunday school. Kids whose parents had moved to Vermont to escape the rat race. Kids with different sensibilities than me and my friends. They knew about city things, had been to places I had never heard of. They played tennis and soccer instead of football. They had money.

We didn't think anything of it then. The new residents became our neighbors and our friends. What we didn't realize at the time was that these people were the pioneers of change, coming at first in dribs and drabs from the cities and suburbs but then in a steady wave, buying up all the land they could get their hands on. My mother's mother, a lifelong Windsor resident, never felt comfortable visiting us in Woodstock. She said the town was too snooty for her likes, full of fancy homes and uppity people. To a certain degree she was right. Woodstock has always been an enclave for the well-to-do. The magnificent colonial houses lining the green in the center of the village are a testament to the prosperity and money that has existed in the town since the eighteenth century.

But my grandmother never saw the Woodstock I did as a boy growing up there. We lived on a small farm about a mile from the village. My father raised beef cattle. My mother had some horses. My brother and I did the chores. Woodstock then was a cozy small town where everyone knew everyone else. I felt secure riding my bike through the village, seeing the same faces each day. The smell of cow manure used to fill the air on summer evenings after the farmers around town had fertilized their hay fields, drifting up and over the Ottauquechee River valley. It was a smell that I loved because it reminded me of my grandparents' farm. It is a smell that has been missing from Woodstock for a long time now. The farms are gone. Woodstock is a tourist town. Tourists do not understand the smell of cow manure; they come to Vermont to see the cows and the green pastures, not to smell the manure.

About the same time the first newcomers were starting to arrive, Laurance Rockefeller decided to make Woodstock into a modern resort town, preserving its historic beauty for posterity, as his father, John D., Jr, had done in colonial Williamsburg. He purchased the landmark Woodstock Inn, long the hub of local activity. He ordered the majestic Victorian structure demolished. A new, cold neocolonial building was erected in its place. The local golf course and ski area were bought and upgraded, and Woodstock was slowly transformed from a sleepy town with occasional tourists to a destination resort crawling with them.

The changes came rapidly and less subtly while I was in high school. More newcomers appeared each fall. Two male models from New York City bought Cabot's paint shop and converted it into a booming discotheque that kept the sidewalks from being rolled up at night. People staying at the Woodstock Inn liked what they saw and began looking around for property to buy. The Morgans' plumbing fixture store became a boutique. Property values started to climb. The farms began to close. The John Deere dealership where my father took our tractor for repairs was bulldozed to make a parking lot for the new inn. Real estate agents seemed drawn to Woodstock like the faithful to Lourdes. About the time Mr. Rockefeller was spending huge sums of money to have the "unsightly" utility lines in the village buried, Woodstock's first trailer park appeared on the fringes west of town. By the time I left for college, the bus tours had started to arrive. The expensive bed and breakfasts and the highbrow art galleries would soon follow.

One day this summer I made one of my rare excursions into Woodstock from the small farm my wife and I caretake in North Pomfret. I don't like going into Woodstock anymore because I find the traffic and the crowds of tourists insufferable. While my wife ran some errands, I stood uneasily in front of a store that sells trinkets to tourists that used to be the barber shop where I got my hair cut when I was a kid. The barber's chair used to sit in the bay of a large storefront window, in full view of people walking past. My friends would stand outside the window and make fun of me while I was getting my hair cut, making faces, trying to crack me up. I remembered those faces and smiled to myself, then looked into the window and saw a display of music boxes hand-made in Vermont. I stood in front of the old barber shop for nearly an hour and did not recognize a soul. Strangers all. Or perhaps I am the one who is now a stranger in my own hometown.

If the forces of change were at work in Woodstock when I was in high school, they were on a second shift in the neighboring town of Quechee. A group of out-of-state developers had bought up thousands of acres of farm- and forestland there and were in the process of building condominiums, vacation homes, two golf courses, tennis courts, a ski area, and a sports center. The goal was to construct the finest second-home development in the country— Quechee Lakes. The developers were operating on the assumption that not everyone wanted to renovate a farmhouse to enjoy Vermont. People from the cities would come to the country if the country was more like the city, if they could occupy themselves with urban activities in a pastoral setting. They were right. The condos sold like hotcakes.

A friend of mine who grew up in Quechee before Quechee Lakes, told me they used to be able to play several innings of uninterrupted softball on Main Street. The change that he was witness to in his hometown dwarfed what I was seeing in Woodstock. The entire character, the soul of Quechee was being altered by developers who re-created the Vermont hamlet in their own citified image. Some cellar holes at a condominium construction site were blown up one summer's night. Word was that a renegade group had formed a latter-day Green Mountain Boys in an attempt to fight the rape of the land that was going on in Quechee. I cheered their bravado and secretly wished I could join them. But the defenders of Vermont's honor were spitting into the winds of change. The vandalism ran its course. The condos went up unabated, spreading like mushrooms in wet weather. Quechee was gone. And they no longer play softball on Main Street.

My first year at the University of Vermont, I lived in a brick shoe box of a dormitory on the far end of campus. My floor was a mixture of in-state and out-of-state students. One of the freshmen who lived next door to me grew up on a farm in the Northeast Kingdom and was able to pass a quarter through his high school class ring without the coin touching the sides, a feat made possible by years of milking cows. The first time we shook hands, his grip reminded me of my grandfather's. My new neighbor was one of nine children and the first in his family to attend college. He wanted to become a lawyer.

One night some of us were sitting around, drinking beers, and talking. Eventually the conversation drifted away from Nixon and Watergate and on to the development that was going on in Vermont. I said I thought the state was in the process of being ruined and that Vermonters were losing control over their home. There were some nods of agreement from the other in-state students. But one of the other students, who had recently moved to Vermont and whose father was making a killing in the burgeoning real estate market at Killington, looked at me and said: "If it weren't for us coming in and buying up your land, Vermonters would be living in tar paper shacks. We are doing you a favor. Besides," he added smugly, "no one is forcing anyone to sell out."

The room fell silent. All eyes turned to our burly classmate with the thick fingers, expecting a fight. But he simply put down his beer and walked quietly from the room. I screamed bloody murder, venting the rage that had been buried inside me since the day the bulldozers arrived on my grandparents' farm. Despite my impassioned protests, the newcomer remained convinced that the development of Vermont was nothing but good. I later asked my neighbor from the Northeast Kingdom why he hadn't taken a stand. He looked down at his class ring and shrugged, "I don't live in a tar paper shack," he said with quiet logic. "Never have and never will."

Several years ago, a friend and I were putting together a television documentary about development in Vermont and went to visit Theron Boyd on his farm in Quechee. Theron was the only farmer not to sell out to the Quechee Lakes development. The developers tried to hoodwink Theron into selling them his land, saying they wanted to raise a few horses next door. He threw them off and told them not to come back. His farm is now a thirty-acre oasis, surrounded by golf courses, tennis courts, and luxury condominiums. We found Theron in his garden. His pale white kneecaps were starting to poke through his blue overalls. Sweat stains ringed his straw hat, marking his days of toil like high-water marks on the banks of a river after a heavy rain. Three quarters of a century of farming and living in a homestead that hadn't been modernized since his family built it 200 years before had left Theron stooped and weathered. Yet his eyes were straight and feisty.

Leery of strangers on his land, Theron was reluctant to talk to me. But after we established that he used to buy cattle from my grandfather, he opened up. He asked after my grandfather. I told him about the interstate and my grandfather's death years ago. Theron had heard about the big highway but had never actually driven on it. In the last twenty years, the only time he left his farm was to drive the few miles to White River to get supplies.

We watched as two men in a golf cart darted past the house and headed off toward a cluster of condos across the road. I asked Theron if he resented his new neighbors. The question seemed to catch him off guard, as if he had never thought about his feelings toward the people in the golf carts. He considered for a moment, then shook his head slowly.

"No," he drawled in a thick Vermont accent. "I don't resent 'em. I feel sorry for 'em."

"Why?" I asked.

"Feel sorry for anyone who doesn't have anything better to do than chase a little white ball around," he said. "They ought to plant a garden and see what it is to grow something."

"How many offers have you had to sell?" I asked.

Theron laughed. "Stopped keepin' track years ago."

For a moment I was standing back at Romaine Tenny's smouldering cellar hole. There were no bulldozers in sight, but the forces of change were as surely aimed at Theron Boyd's farm. Like Romaine Tenny, the land, his farm, his way of life meant everything to Theron. He would never sell, he told me. But without family to pass his farm along to, Theron regretted that someday the condos would stand there. We talked to Theron a while longer and left him in his garden pulling beets for his supper.

In the spring of 1978, I was headed home from Washington, D.C., after an unsuccessful attempt at city living. Most of my friends had left Vermont to seek their fortunes and I followed the tide, only to find I felt miserably out of place in the city. As I sat in a frenzied traffic jam on the George Washington Bridge, with New York City peering out through the smog below, it seemed that I couldn't get back to Vermont fast enough.

The traffic on Interstate 91 thinned out north of Springfield, past Northampton, where the road begins to wind along the Connecticut River. I felt a rush of excitement as I crossed the Massachusetts border into Vermont south of Brattleboro, the feeling I always get when returning home after being away for long. Soon my grandparents' farm appeared before me, fallow. I pulled off on Exit 9, once our cornfield. The barns and farmhouse across the road looked shabby. The fields beyond the interstate had filled with weeds. The lawn by the house was overrun with dandelions. I thought how sad my grandparents would be to see their farm now.

My spirits buoyed again as I headed up the Skunk Hollow toward Woodstock. I was excited about being home again and being able to walk the fields and woodlands I had roamed when I was growing up. While I was in the city, I had longed to sit atop the field in the back forty, where the noise of Route 4 subsides, and contemplate the hills beyond the Ottauquechee Valley. I wondered if our apple orchard next to the pond was in bloom as I pulled onto the short dirt road a mile east of town that climbs to an open plateau above the Ottauquechee River facing our farm. I looked to my right, across one of our hay fields, toward our neighbor's farm, and what I saw made me feel sick. My foot involuntarily stomped on the brake peddle. The car skidded to a halt. Four immense cellar holes gaped in the ground in the field next to our house. The last time I saw the field there were cows grazing in it. There had always been cows in it.

My mother was waiting for me, knowing what my reaction would be. She told me our neighbor had sold part of his farm to a developer who was building twenty-four luxury condominiums. The same dread I felt when my grandparents' farm was destroyed swept over me. I didn't know who I should be angry at. Our neighbor for selling out? The developer for raping the land? My parents for not doing something about it?

"How could you let this happen?" I snapped.

"How could we stop it?" my mother replied, masking her own frustration. "It won't be so bad," she added, trying to sound optimistic. "The developer promises we won't even notice them. He's going to plant trees."

I stared at the last of the four cellar holes, fifty feet from our fence line, a hundred yards from our house. Even with trees, I knew we would notice these condominiums very well indeed.

My anger grew with the condominiums. The noise and dust from construction filled the summer air. Foundations climbed out of the cellar holes. A skeleton of wood formed. Sun decks and skylights were attached. The workmen moved inside to install the guts. Units one and two were finally done. They looked out of place, as though, embarrassed by their presence, the land was trying to distance itself from the buildings.

But the view from the sun decks of the condos of our farm and the Ottauquechee River was spectacular, and soon cars carrying potential buyers started arriving to investigate. There were no Vermont plates on those cars. They were from Massachusetts, New York, Connecticut, New Jersey.

Our first new neighbors moved into unit one and immediately started walking their dogs and having nature picnics in our fields and woods. It was more than I could bear. I went out and bought the brightest fluorescent paint I could find, the screaming orange variety. On a four-by-eight-foot piece of plywood I painted NO TRESPASSING!! USE OF THIS LAND NOT INCLUDED WITH CONDO!!! in large, angry letters. I dragged the sign into the field next to the condos and hammered it onto posts like a billboard. The sign was the first thing prospective buyers would see as they drove in. It was visible for several hundred yards. It glowed in the dark. I walked back to the house pleased with the notion that our new neighbors might think they had moved in next door to a maniac.

The call came immediately.

"What's the deal with the sign?" the developer's lawyer complained to my mother.

"We want things to be clear," she said uncomfortably.

"I'll make sure our salespeople tell the buyers," he promised. "No need for the sign. It's an eyesore."

"My son says you should plant trees like you promised," she said, her easygoing nature eroding. "We think your condos are the eyesore."

There was a pause on the other end of the line. "All right," the developer's lawyer finally snapped. "Just take down the sign."

I disassembled the billboard and waited for the trees. Foliage season arrived but the trees didn't. More condos were finished. But no trees. The newcomers would assemble on their sun decks with their friends for cocktails and point out the geography of their vista. I could see a man in bright green corduroys, a drink in one hand, tracing the hills beyond our barn in the air with his free hand.

On Columbus Day, when several leaf peepers were perusing the condos, I put the sign back up. With deer season fast approaching, I took to sighting-in my rifle in the field below the condos just around cocktail hour when the new neighbors appeared on the sun deck to take in the view. The repeated crack of a .308 rebounding through the settling dusk air had an unnerving effect. These people had clearly not moved to Vermont to hear the sound of gunfire. By early November the trees arrived. Small red pines. I dragged the sign back out of the field and stopped sighting-in my rifle.

The condos are now all completed, twenty-four in all. Many of the red pines have since died. Those that are left will, in another twenty or thirty years, start to screen the buildings from view.

I hope my family still owns our farm in twenty or thirty years—even in three years—but the pressures to sell are enormous. The real estate market in the area has made the land too valuable. Taxes are high. Upkeep is a problem for my mother, who lives alone now. Developers salivate when they see our farm. It is one of the largest parcels of land left close to the village of Woodstock that is not owned by Mr. Rockefeller. My mother has had offers. She does not want to sell the land. She hangs on. For now.

There is a flat piece of ground on a ridge above the farm where I have long dreamed of building my home and raising my family. The wild crab apple trees and the hemlocks open into a sunny clearing. It is a fine place for a home. But before I can afford to build, my mother may have to sell all or part of the farm. If she does, the land will probably not be bought by another Vermonter. It will likely be purchased by a land developer, who will spin it off into ten-acre lots and put up expensive homes. Or maybe it will be bought by an investment banker with money to burn who will renovate the house, put in a tennis court and swimming pool, and use the place as his country retreat in fashionable Woodstock. If my mother has to sell, another Vermont family will have lost deed to its heritage.

I think often of my grandparents. They would not understand Vermont today. Passing along a farm or land from generation to generation was the way things were done then. But they lived in a time before renovated farmhouses, destination resorts, and condominiums. Vermonters like Romaine Tenny and Theron Boyd are a dying breed. With them gone, Vermont's soul disappears. It is too late to save my hometown. But maybe it isn't too late to save my mother's farm and preserve a small piece of Vermont as well as a legacy for my family. If not, I hope I can well enough remember what Vermont was like to tell my children. Or perhaps I can get on Interstate 91 and drive north past St. Johnsbury and show them the Northeast Kingdom before it, too, is changed forever.

Aged in Vermont

Lee Pennock Huntington

The tradition of longevity in my father's family is long-lived. His great-great-grandfather, James Pennock, "the first to break the soil" of Strafford, Vermont, in 1768, died at the age of ninety-six; his wife, Thankful, mother of eleven, lived to be eighty-one. The widowed mother of James, an English clergyman's daughter, came in her seventies to join her son in the Vermont wilderness, bringing, it is said, Bible, prayer book, and linen tablecloths to grace the "pumpkin pine table." She spent her old age there in apparent contentment with her children, grandchildren, and great-grand-children, leading the family in Sunday services in the forest until a church could be built. Despite its rigors, Vermont was then, and still is, I believe, not a bad place to grow old.

Not that anyone actually looks forward to aging. Benjamin Franklin put it bluntly when he observed, "all would live long, but none would grow old." With the onset of years, some accommodation with the inevitable has to be made, and whether or not it is successful has a lot to do with the sort of society in which one does the graying. In a nation that idolizes youth, vigor, and sexual attraction, there is widespread horror of aging, a frantic effort to fend it off and disguise it. The fact that medical miracles can now keep us going far beyond the average life span of the past does not bring automatic happiness to the burgeoning population of elders today. They are not guaranteed the respect, affection, employment opportunities, or decent physical care that can compensate in some measure for declining powers. This is especially the case in urban areas, where all too many old people live in loneliness and neglect, cast off by a heedless society.

Vermont, by contrast, is a more hospitable climate for what are euphemistically called the golden years. It has indubitably something to do with living with mountains. They are secure, abiding, their permanence reassuring, giving tangible perspective to human affairs. When I must be away from them for any length of time, a definite unease takes over spirit and body. In a very real sense I can feel the metabolism change for the better, an actual uplifting, once I return. Days spent in the presence of hills are days well spent if one listens to what they are saying. This is something Vermonters instinctively know, and it surely has its positive effect upon the way one responds to the challenges of aging.

Then too, Vermont has a great advantage over other regions in its scale, which is comfortingly human. There are no monstrous blighted cities, no vast uninhabited areas. Villages of less than a thousand dot the map, and they are not far distant from one another. The faces of your neighbors are familiar and usually friendly. You are likely to know your state legislators and to feel reasonably confident that if you write to your senator his response will not be entirely impersonal. The governor makes an effort to be accessible. An authentic sense of cohesion can be discerned throughout the population, whatever the differences of politics or income, a conviction that this small proud state really is different from the other forty-nine. In a word, it is a place and a society that is distinctly less intimidating than many others, where people, including the old, have a better chance of knowing each other, of feeling secure and at home.

That is not to say that all is idyllic in the Green Mountains. Our cities may be small and few, but even so there are festering pockets of destitution. Traversing the rural regions, you see not just magnificent scenery, prosperous resorts, neat villages and farmhouses, but also old shacks surrounded by disemboweled autos and cast-off appliances, the dark side of the picturesque. I have known of old people holed up in miserable dwellings that would horrify a health inspector—noxious kerosene heaters in the kitchen and privies decaying out in back; the best that can be said of such housing is that the inhabitants are not actually homeless.

Yet I still argue that by and large it really is better to age in Vermont, even in a third-hand trailer or a drafty farmhouse that hasn't had any particular maintenance for a hundred years, than it is to live anonymously in an impersonal city or to retire among strangers in the Sun Belt.

The difference is people and a tradition of unobtrusive helpfulness. It used to be, and not so very far in the past, that the indigent and unfortunate would be taken care of by the town, assigned to the poorhouse or farmed out by the selectmen, with every penny spent recorded in the annual Town Report for every voter to inspect. This was charity for which few wished to be eligible, and insofar as possible, families took care of their own. Although today a good many basic needs are assumed by Social Security, Medicare and Medicaid, food stamps, fuel allotments, and a battery of social service agencies, Vermonters are aware there are other needs. Here families, friends, neighbors express their concern for the older generation in ways that often reveal a high order of sensitivity along with the pragmatic.

Once I shared a hospital room with a gallant grandmother fighting breast cancer. Medical expenses were to a large extent taken over by Medicare, but the support of her large family was a textbook example of the kind of devotion all elderly patients would pray to experience and which I have witnessed many times in Vermont. It was a small hospital where there was no nonsense about prohibiting visitors under the age of twelve, so during the afternoon grandchildren were brought to her bedside, and babies crowed cheerfully from their mothers' laps. After school the teenagers came, the gangly lads inarticulate but the girls talkative and helpful about arranging their grandmother's pillows and fetching ice water. In the evening after farm chores, her husband came in shyly to sit beside her bed, giving her, in concise phrases, a report on the day's events in field and barn. Her tall sons arrived to stand against the wall, making family jokes among themselves, while their wives bustled about changing water in flower vases, talking brightly to their mother-in-law of households and offspring. Sisters and brothers made frequent appearances, bearing chocolates and magazines. That blessed woman was in no doubt of her continuing importance to her family, and she knew hers was not a battle of isolation.

Not everyone, of course, has such an extended family to count on when hospitalized, but I've noticed that those who may have less in the way of kin, or perhaps are even solitary, will not be neglected by neighbors and friends, who make a point of visiting, telephoning, bringing little gifts and assurances of concern. If an octogenarian insists upon living on in the old homestead, there are almost invariably neighbors or relatives who keep an eye on him, bringing in the groceries, checking on the woodpile and the chicken feed. They will note if the kitchen light is left on all day and will drop in to see whether Uncle Harvey has just forgotten to turn it off or has fallen down the cellar stairs and broken his hip. If there is a fracture or a case of pneumonia, help is at hand, beginning with the volunteer ambulance crew. There are excellent medical centers throughout the state and physicians who may even pay house calls. In the last resort, there are nursing homes. Wherever, these are never jolly places to visit, but those I have seen in Vermont are clean, well run, and staffed by solicitous people. Some of them even offer the comfort of views of the everlasting hills.

We hear a disturbing lot these days about elderly abuse and neglect, and this can happen in Vermont, though mercifully not with frequency. A brother allows his recluse sister to freeze to death in the filth of her collapsing house. A niece purloins her addled old uncle's pension check. But such deeds, when they come to light, arouse real public outrage. They are considered a disgrace not only to the human race but to Vermont, which prides itself on fair treatment. The motto of this state is "Freedom and Unity." Freedom to live and let live, but unity in standing together against injustice.

The concern for one's neighbor, especially if the neighbor is elderly, is finding new implementation these days. It goes beyond the customary bringing 'round of casseroles in cases of crisis. There are now organized efforts to meet specific situations. Support groups for cancer patients and families of Alzheimer's disease victims are functioning effectively, and hospice groups are doing their work of compassion in every part of the state. In the town I know best, a concerted endeavor over several years of consultation, thoughtful planning, fund-raising, and trial and error has resulted in a Community Care program with a salaried director and dozens of dedicated volunteers young, old, and in-between. It provides the kind of practical help that makes all the difference, with countless hours of tending to the needs of the sick, handicapped, lonely, or helpless and giving respite to care givers. An adult day-care center has been established, and there is a campaign afoot to convert the inn on the green—which has a history of leaving too many hopeful owners bankrupt—into supervised living quarters for those who can no longer manage on their own, enabling them to stay in the community as long as possible. Elsewhere a few retirement communities have sprung up for those who can afford it, and I would guess that they would offer more satisfaction than those among the palm trees.

It's my conviction that Vermont is a healthy place for all ages, with particular benefits for the elderly. I even recommend the climate, despite its well-known challenges. I believe it was a Swedish study that demonstrated more alertness in citizens of regions where there are distinct seasonal changes, requiring physical and psychological adjustments that contribute to adaptability to other changes in life. Aging certainly requires adjustments, and Vermont weather certainly provides practice in meeting dramatic changes, not simply in year-round cycles but from day to day, even, as we've all experienced, from hour to hour. True, there are Vermonters who gratefully retire to Florida, vowing never to endure another prolonged siege of blizzards, icy roads, snow shoveling, canceled appointments, and acute arthritis. (They do tend to come back with the swallows, though, to visit their relatives and drive— slowly—through the hills and valleys to savor again the freshness and the green.) On the other hand, what is probably a majority of Vermonters prefers the bracing northern climate, speaking slightingly of a retreat to the tropics. These hardy characters take a perverse pride in remaining through the winter, determined to meet its mandates as long as they live, positively invigorated by near-zero temperatures. Mostly, though, they sensibly modify their routines to take into account diminished physical abilities, mindful of what one slip on the icy doorstep can entail, and I know several people of advanced years who put their cars up on blocks from Thanksgiving to Easter.

Everyone has heard the old tales about grandpa and grandma being stored away in the woodshed for the winter, to be thawed out in the spring, but no one has ever produced documentation of such drastic measures, so we must credit those stories to the famous Vermont humor that combines a recognition of stark realities with a robust taste for exaggeration. When house space was minimal, central heating nonexistent, and winter provisions limited, the presence of the old folks could well become a burden, as they themselves were surely aware. But many are the true stories of families of yore sitting around the hearth in harmony, with grandfather whittling pegs and grandmother knitting while the children listened to them tell tales of pioneer days, of catamounts and hailstorms, Indians and floods, the battles of Bennington and Bull Run, while the wind whipped around the house and snow piled up to the sills. The oldest members living on in a household expected to be and were expected to be of help as long as they were able, participating in whatever farm tasks they could still handle, tending babies, mending harness, cracking butternuts, and peeling apples, knowing themselves useful in some way until they dropped. The work ethic never has had an age limit in Vermont.

Now that farms are vanishing at an alarming rate and young families have trouble finding affordable housing, such gatherings of generations under one roof are increasingly rare. Grandparents, great-aunts and uncles, elderly cousins often nowadays live quite separately, in a tiny apartment or a mobile home, their walls decked with photographs of the scattered younger members of the family. But they keep in touch. It is not quite the heartbreaking sundering that took place during the great nineteenth-century out-migration, when thousands of westbound Vermonters bade a final farewell to the old folks on the worn-out hill farms, but it is, for those who must today live alone in their old age, a different situation from the best of what it was in the way of togetherness in the past.

There are many reminders of change. In addition to the inescapable deterioration of eyesight and hearing, the creaking of bones and the aching of joints, the irregularities of heartbeat and the disturbing lapses of memory, the ever-present specter of cancer or stroke, there are changes within the surroundings that weigh upon the elderly, bringing a different kind of stress. It is a profound loss to see the farms of one's youth no longer producing, fields and meadows grown up to brush or sprouting condominiums, towns and villages expanding yearly with the arrival of more and more strangers. Having been intimately involved in "the environment" all their lives, although it was never called that in their youth, they know better than any newcomers how it needs protection. It hurts to see forests eaten by acid rain, landfills overflowing, streams polluted, strip developments disfiguring roadsides, discount houses proliferating in quiet country towns. They know the ski resorts and second homes provide jobs, enabling some to remain who might otherwise leave, but these are service jobs, usually low paying and with little future. Meanwhile, other old-timers may be frustrated by state environmental legislation preventing sale of their property, often their only capital, to developers. In the Northeast Kingdom particularly, whole towns have risen to protest laws perceived as antithetical to sacred rights of personal property. It will take all the wisdom of both old and young to solve these problems. With age, deaths, and economics calling the tune, there are inevitably many uprootings from the long-familiar to new settings, new rules and standards. Such metamorphoses in the public and private spheres can be profoundly disturbing, sometimes threatening one's very identity. Yet I have seen great courage in the face of the most disruptive shifts, a determination to keep up a good front, lacing complaints with humor. These are stalwarts who exemplify Paul Klee's dictum for architecture: to stand, despite all possibility to fall.

Aren't there old curmudgeons, whiners, and nervous Nellies in Vermont? To be sure, but they don't strike me as typical. And it often seems as if outlanders who choose to come here in retirement handle their advancing years in much the same spirit as the native Vermonters, either because they arrive with the right stuff or they acquire it from example once they get here. We're not talking now about those who opt for the luxurious enclaves put up by developers, complete with saunas and golf courses, for people who prize the scenery but never get to know the "locals." It is those who settle in the country or towns, run useful small businesses, or go into modest farming enterprises who can fit in very comfortably, making real contributions to the community. The old-timers may lament, "I don't know anybody when I go downstreet any more," but they can see that the newcomers are helping to revive the economy and are enlivening cultural life.

In this atypical corner of a youth-oriented society, there is still general respect for elders. They are not segregated or ignored but continue to be active and influential in local affairs, serving as selectmen, on school boards, and in civic organizations and taking on multiple church responsibilities well beyond early old age. They may not have read Simone de Beauvoir's massive study, *The Coming of Age*, but they practice what she preaches: "There is only one solution if old age is not to be an absurd parody of our former life, and that is to go on pursuing ends that give our existence a meaning—devotion to individuals, to groups or causes, social, political, intellectual or creative work. One's life has value so long as one attributes value to the life of others, by means of love, friendship, indignation, compassion." They are highly visible and vocal members of the community, present and participating in all town events. In one cherished segment of our culture, there could hardly be a covered-dish supper or a bake sale without the offerings of the seniors. At school plays and ceremonies, if you are counting heads in the audience, a goodly portion will be found to be gray or white; their interest in all the members of the up-coming generation is intense and personal.

With young people launched into a brave new world of high technology, its very vocabulary a barrier between generations, a continuity of culture is difficult to sustain. Old knowledge, old traditions no longer have the usefulness, the life-preserving, identity-fortifying patterns of what Margaret Mead called post-figurative culture, dependent upon experienced oldsters for the passing on of social imperatives to their descendants. Yet what the parents and grandparents can and do still give to following generations is a set of values. The virtue of hard, honest work. The standard of self-reliance. The necessity of helping one's neighbors. Setting examples in their own lives, the old conserve an essential continuity of behavior in a dramatically changing world. As Florida Scott-Maxwell writes in *The Measure of My Days*, the marvelous journal she kept in her eighty-third year, "The last years may matter most."

Even arriving at the nineties does not necessarily mean calling it quits. I have several friends in that select category who are carrying on with undiminished appetite for life. They tend their gardens, drive their automobiles, go to meetings and lectures, travel, speak up in Town Meeting, attend gatherings of families and friends and welcome them to their own homes. One dear friend takes her sketchbook everywhere, paints luminous landscapes in her studio, and fires up her kiln whenever she has whipped up a good batch of her imaginative ceramics. With unquenchable enthusiasm she embraces friends of all ages and greets any exigency with her trademark phrase, "What the heck!" And then there is George Seldes, that indomitable investigative journalist who came to Vermont in his sixties, now in his 100th year contemplating yet another book, this one titled *To Hell with the Joys of Old Age*.

Keeping up a good front is not the same thing as tinkering with appearances. Substance has long held priority over semblance in Vermont, and this extends to the literal face one presents to the world. I had an example in my great-aunt Winifred, whom I was taken to visit when I was about fourteen. Aunt Winifred, one of eleven children (this family was still taking seriously the biblical injunction on begetting), had lived all her life on the family farm, assuming responsibility for four younger brothers who never married. In her seventies she was, I thought, what was meant by "lively as a cricket." Slender and erect, blue eyes sparkling, cheeks rosy, white hair tucked in a bun, in her immaculate pink gingham dress she looked fresh and amazingly youthful. When my father ventured a gentle compliment, she demurred. "No, Gilbert, I've gotten to the stage where I don't care to look in the mirror any longer. Nothing to be done about it." Then she looked at me, her eyes sharp but affectionate, seeing right into my adolescent vanity and preoccupation with how I appeared to the world, especially boys.

"You know," she said, "when I was your age, I was the prettiest girl in town." Then she paused, twinkling mischievously, and added dryly, "Of course, there were only three of us."

That, I thought, is the way to be when you are old. Neat, active, sense of humor intact, no pretenses.

Simone de Beauvoir wrote, "I have never come across one single woman, either in life or in books, who has looked upon her own old age cheerfully." Cheerful or not, Vermont women seem less fixated on disguising their years than their city sisters. Skinny or stout, they do not try to look like teenagers. They seem comfortable with their figures and clothe them with little regard for the latest in fashion. They are exceedingly neat or contentedly untidy. It is seldom that one of them will dye her hair or even resort to cosmetics, and if there is an old lady with a face-lift in Vermont, I haven't met her. This acceptance of the inevitable in wear and tear was traditional in previous generations of Vermonters—just look at those old daguerreotypes—and is still honored here, though perhaps it will die out one day. As far as the males are concerned, I personally find the old men of Vermont almost always pleasing to look upon, their faces lined with life and lit with wry humor. Still garbed in their working outfits, checked flannel shirts, boots, and billed caps, they manage to look the world in the eye whatever their physical afflictions.

When I was in grade school, on our report cards there was, below the lines for marks in arithmetic, spelling, and penmanship, a space labeled ATTITUDE, where the teacher could write comments on cooperativeness, sharing, effort, playground behavior, and so on. Some of the brightest pupils whose academic showings were commendable did not receive rave reviews on attitude. They were too independent, too interested in the world outside the classroom, not reliably docile. If the elders of Vermont, a good many of them anyway, were graded today on attitude, it would be precisely those nonconformist traits that might be shown to make them successful in their dealings with the exigencies of age. They are not going gently into oblivion but instead are meeting each day with agendas for work and activities that matter to them and communication on whatever levels they choose. Not for them relegation to corners to sit watching endless mindless television programs geared to the lowest common denominator. They are geared to involvement in the stream of life as long as they are physically and mentally capable.

The very thought of ever having to slow down fills me with defiance. I fully intend to go on forever doing everything I'm doing now plus a host of things I haven't gotten around to yet. Still, reality creeps in on these presumptuous manifestos as I see all around me the de-escalations enforced by eroded bodies and fading minds. A valiant friend who kept her wits about her well into her nineties, as she compared herself with her contemporaries down the line, used to chortle gleefully, "Thank the Lord I still have all my marbles." Marble keeping of course is not something decided by simple resolve. It has a great deal to do with genes and luck, and all the positive thinking and deliberate maintenance of healthful habits and lively interests in the world cannot protect against the onslaughts of disease and accidents. There's no use pretending that one is invulnerable to the slings and arrows that multiply with age.

In rural areas there is a recognition by elders of the ineluctable fact that death, if not actually imminent, is as much a reality on the horizon as today's sunset or next autumn's dismantling of the leafy glory of the hills. I have seen a fine stoic acceptance of this on the part of many old people, right up to the final days of a long illness. For the survivors, knowing not who comes next, there can even be a dark humor, as in the case of Lawrence Fenn, the epitome of the birthright Vermonter.

Lawrence sold his all-purpose farm after his wife died, but he keeps his sugar bush, his ample vegetable patch, his woodlot, and his skill as a mason. Working tirelessly on our barn foundation, he would take a few moments off from time to time to tell us about the hops that used to be grown on our place or to point out a wasp nest abuilding in the eaves. One day I made a discreet attempt to discover Lawrence's age, but he was cagey.

"Old enough," was all he would say. Then he launched into one of his inimitable anecdotes. "Puts me in mind of Henry Perkins and Milton Tracy. They were at the cemetery for the funeral of George Allen, friend of theirs. George got a proper burial and when it was over, Henry said to Milt, 'Milt, how old are you?'"

Here Lawrence's voice took on the high trembling note of the extreme aged. "Milt told him, 'Ninety-seven.'

"They stood there in the graveyard for some minutes, and then Milt said, 'How old are you, Henry?' And Henry told him, 'Ninety-six.'

"They stood there some more, not too long, it had started to snow, and then Milt said, 'Hardly pays us to go home, do it?'"

It may be that I cherish too rosy a view of what after all is a complex mix of attitudes and situations, good and bad. It is clearly a mistake to think of Vermont as a paradise for the old, for no place is, and I do know that Robert Browning's blithe invitation, "Grow old along with me, The best is yet to be," rings hollow for many of the aged. The Swiss philosopher Henri Amiel put it well: "To know how to grow old is the master-work of wisdom, and one of the most difficult chapters in the great art of living." I can only suggest that, for some, that difficult chapter may be lived here with less stress and disappointment than in many other locales.

For myself, I know that when sobering reflections on the intimations of mortality come to mind, I still find comfort in the prospect of meeting these nemeses on my own ground, here where I belong, here where the cycles of nature teach us daily, seasonally, something about inevitability and acceptance. This is the place I want to be in my old age, the place where on every hand can be seen the possibility of beauty and endurance, not mere survival, in the process of growing into age. To become, God willing, not everlasting, but old, as the hills.

To Hell with the Homestead!

Geof Hewitt

The other day our washing machine broke down. I fiddled with it for ten minutes, then phoned one of those sole-proprietor repair services that provides part of the essential fabric of life in Vermont, you know, a business run out of a shop in the garage with a proprietor who still makes house calls and charges about half what our citified retail/repair shops demand. It was Sunday morning: I left my message on a tape machine. Dennis Roberts, the owner-repairman, returned my call late that afternoon and told me how to remove the cover from the washing machine to check for problems I might solve without his help.

"Look for a sock in the pump," he said. "The pump is housed in transparent plastic, so you'll see the sock if it's there."

As I hunkered in the damp cellar with a flashlight in one hand and a screwdriver in the other, removing the cover with surprising ease, I realized that never before in my life had I ever had to deal with a broken-down washing machine.

I grew up in a house that didn't have such an appliance—the laundry was "sent out"—and until ten years ago, when Janet and I moved with our children, Anna and Ben, to our tidy little Cape house in the country, we used local Laundromats or a washtub.

Ben's diapers were washed in a plastic garbage can with a hole cut in the lid through which we gyrated a toilet plunger. That was seventeen years ago: We were living the simple life. Anna, now nearly twelve, spent most of her infancy in disposable diapers, during the period we made weekly trips to the Laundromat.

Janet grew up on a farm in southern Iowa and will never consent to surroundings any less rural than those we presently have; I'm from suburban New Jersey. How did we get to Vermont, such a "faraway place" in the minds of our hometown and college friends? And why is it, in such rural splendor, that Janet and I both seem to be "pursuing careers," maintaining two automobiles, and sitting around the dinner table as a family only two or three times a week? Such an important concern in the last couple of decades, our "lifestyle" seems no different from that of the young nuclear family in southern Iowa or suburban New Jersey, except, because we live ten miles out of town, a tiny town at that, there's little choice of repair shops when the modern appliance ceases to function.

In 1968, I bought an old farm in East Enosburg. The barn had blown down a few years earlier, the owners were in their mid-sixties, and their son had no interest in farming. I was in graduate school, teaching English at the University of Iowa and plotting a way to drop out, taking whatever little work I'd need to provide the few necessities I couldn't produce for myself. Why, I could buy a good horse, so I wouldn't even need an automobile!

In 1970, I "settled" in Vermont, moving into the East Enosburg farmhouse, seven miles by dirt road from the village of Enosburg Falls. I decided that a horse could wait and, as summer gave way to a cooler season, forgot the notion entirely.

It seems obvious to me now, as I feign objectivity in reviewing the choices I made in the days when Woodstock still represented a fresh spirit, that I was intent on participating in the solution to society's problems. Influenced by Thoreau, Helen and Scott Nearing, and by then-current books like *The Making of a Counter-Culture*, *The Greening of America*, and *Small is Beautiful*, I knew there were simply too many liberal artsy people like me flooding the job markets. Why should I compete when I had so much to learn about the physical and natural world; I didn't even know how hens get pregnant or whether that was required for them to produce eggs!

Part of the impulse that drew me to homesteading was the lure of something for nothing. Turning my own labor into meeting my needs would help remove me from the millions of people who are taxed on income they quickly use for the amenities I could provide for myself.

To Hell with the Homestead!   **157**

But most important, I had fallen in love with Vermont. I wanted to be where the air and water were clean, where forestland and open spaces were more common than human settlements, where communities were strong because the population is small enough that every person matters. I wanted to live simply and to make a difference. There were other places, I knew, that met those criteria, but for years I had been visiting my brothers and sisters — Vermont residents for a long time. I knew Vermont well enough to relish all four of its seasons, and I wanted to be near my family.

Through an odd and wonderful set of circumstances, Janet and I met shortly after I moved to Enosburg and married six months later. Janet found work milking cows on a neighbor's farm, and I wrote magazine articles and hired out at several schools as a writer-in-residence. We installed an oil, hot-air furnace in the old farmhouse; I built a chimney to accommodate it but didn't know to mix sand with the mortar, so the chimney blocks, hefted up an aluminum extension ladder and heaved into place, formed a chimney shaped a bit like the letter S. That didn't matter, though. Wendell Savage, who grew up in the house, visited one day, looked at the chimney, scratched his chin and said, "I never saw smoke that wouldn't bend."

After three years in the house, we moved out — with Ben, then two years old — into a cabin we were still working on, up at the edge of a meadow, about 800 feet off the road. The cabin had no electricity, no telephone, no indoor plumbing. We took out a subscription to *The Mother Earth News*. I remember telling people we were going to "do more with less."

Members of our family, and friends who were living in suburbia, said they'd thought we already were doing more with less — why did we want to move even farther from civilization?

Well, I'd have explained if anyone was listening, the old house was really too big for us, and it required constant maintenance. The water system was forever freezing in winter and leaking in summer, and I was sick of working on it. One February I had set the kitchen floor on fire with a torch I was using to thaw the pipes.

The following August, my Aunt Dot arrived unexpectedly from New Jersey to find me digging trenches at 100-foot intervals along half a mile of well-buried and long-forgotten water line, first looking for the old lead pipe, then looking for a leak. I'd been at it nearly a week and, without a tub of water to come home to, was clammy to say the least.

"I wish I could offer you something—even a glass of water," I apologized.

We all laughed.

But life in the cabin also required its own maintenance, and through many lessons I learned that "the good life" is often more romantic in theory than in practice.

Garden produce from our too-large plots was always abundant, especially zucchinis. We spent a full week, late one summer, freezing endless containers of watery squash and package after package of milkweed, blanched thrice over a hot plate and thrice drained. Exhorting Janet on a fly-ridden, sweltering, humid afternoon as steam curled about her face, I gloated "Free! It's all free."

A year later I tried to get the hogs to gnash it down.

In addition to the pigs, we kept chickens, a goat, and a couple of geriatric Volkswagens. All but the chickens moved with us to the cabin: They would stay in the shed down by the house until we built them suitable quarters. The pigs used fifty-five-gallon drums for shelter, and the goat was fine in a little temporary shed, but she got to climbing on automobiles and coming into the cabin and broke our favorite sugar jar so we gave her away.

We cooked over construction scraps and kindling foraged from the forest floor just behind our new home. We rented a food locker in town and butchered the pigs. On neighbors' kitchen ranges we prepared our vegetables for freezing. In late August we froze our corn. On one such occasion, I was using an instrument called the "American Corn Cutter," advertised in a mail-order catalog as "the best device we've found," a curved blade set in a piece of molded yellow plastic with slots to hold it in place over a bowl. The victim slides the cob up and down with thumb and four fingers, and on a particularly thin ear of corn my forefinger raked the blade. A piece of my fingerprint, about the size of three kernels, fell into the bowl. After two years the fingertip still went cold a lot sooner than any of my other digits yet was curiously numb the rest of the time.

We built a pole construction shed for the chickens and moved them to their new home, then Janet spent the better part of December putting up tar paper and stapling cardboard over the cracks so they wouldn't freeze. Twice a day, December to March, we replaced the chickens' frozen water trough with one that had been thawed.

Constructing the outhouse was my first completely no-plans project. By the time we'd built the cabin (with a lot of patient help from friends who took on all precision work) and the henhouse (which I managed by myself, with guidance from Garden Way's Pole Construction book), I was fairly at ease with hammer and saw, so using scraps from these projects I set out, in late September, to get us a little comfort. Never mind what we'd been using all summer — with winter coming on, we needed something protected.

Here are two helpful rules for building an outhouse:

1. Dig hole before you build.
2. Don't use hole until house is completed.

I followed these simple rules proudly and within two days the place was ready, except for a door. I've never been much at hinging things, so after I constructed an unabashedly rustic door, I nailed it temporarily shut. Then, with everything stable, I proceeded to screw the hinges in. I'll spare you the details of stripped screws and the ultimate defeat of all bad carpenters, having to use nails in about half the hinge holes. Finally, exhausted, sweating, and out of sorts, I stepped back to eye the completed job — the hinges looked level and fairly tight, in spite of a bent-over nail in one hole and the gleam of angry filings where screws had been abused. I was ready to pull the temporary nails, open the door, and leave the outhouse until I needed it. I could clean up later.

When, with all the nails out, the door was rigid, refusing to open, I was overwhelmed with chagrin. The hinges had been installed backwards. The humor of screwing myself into the outhouse was momentarily lost on me and I bashed the door open. Years later, the outhouse remained without a door. Winter visits were downright numbing, but the view was magnificent. Some nights I actually lingered to watch northern lights I'd have missed if we lived in a "modern house."

One of my few legitimate accomplishments during this time involved installing a water line. Three thousand feet from the cabin, an old spring was our only known reliable source of water. A hill rises between spring and cabin, but from a road half a mile across the valley one can see both the approximate location of the spring and the cabin. The spring looks lower. And, as near as one can pinpoint locations on a topographical map, the cabin is sited in the topographical band that is twenty feet higher than that of the spring. A gravity system would bring the water halfway up our hill, we figured, at least within hauling distance of the cabin, so we bought thirty 100-foot lengths of one-inch plastic pipe and hired Reg Robtoy and his backhoe to dig us a trench. We worked down the hill from the spring, burying the pipe four feet where ledge didn't force a shallower trench, and followed the road around the hill that hides the cabin from the spring. I connected lengths of pipe, eased them into the trench, and shoveled protective layers of sod over them as Reggie dug and backfilled with the machine.

Of course, the water came strong through the pipe as we reached the system's low point. But as anticipated, the water pressure dropped when we started digging through the meadow, up toward the cabin. Every two or three hours we'd be ready to link another hundred-foot section of pipe to the system, and I'd approach the uphill end to find the water emerging ever less enthusiastically. After four hot days we connected the final hundred feet of pipe. I ran to the uphill end, which was oozing water at ground level! Down in the trench it produced a gallon and a half per minute, delivered right to the cabin door. Reggie and I nearly danced.

"I'd have bet the price of this job the water'd never make it up the hill," he said.

Free of power, heat, telephone, and water bills, we lived on $6,000 a year. Two thousand dollars went to mortgage payments and property taxes, $800 paid health and automobile insurance, and $300 covered federal and state taxes. We weren't all that loose with our cash, but we were living the life we had envisioned for ourselves.

Our next building project was a woodshed—again a pole construction job, started in late October with the skies gray and damp winds threatening snow. Friends helped on this job and it was done in a day, up solid if a bit diagonal from where a truck had rammed it during construction.

To Hell with the Homestead!   **161**

Then the job came to fill it—which I did easily by paying $100 for a truckload of sawlogs. I blocked up the logs with a chain saw, then split the wood (and two good axe handles): Our shed was full before the first heavy snows of November. Moreover, we had a nice big pile of extra blocks that I would split come springtime.

By mid-January we were shoveling down through layers of snow to get to the top of that spare pile of wood. February, I went out on skis with chain saw and sled in search of standing dead-wood. A full woodshed is only as good as the woodshed is big. We muddled through the rest of the winter, staying plenty busy during daylight hours, looking forward to the longer days of spring, warming weather, and the pleasures of our garden.

But, to tell the truth, we were a little disenchanted with reading by kerosene lanterns, and the nights were too long! I remember thinking, like a person who hits himself repeatedly on the head with a hammer, that as soon as I quit, things were really going to get good. Then summer was with us, and we forgot the discomforts of winter. This cycle lasted four years.

When we moved to the cabin, Ben was small enough to require little space, young enough that we and a few simple toys were all the diversion he needed. By the time he was five, we would wake to his daily question: Whom could he visit? We marveled that we'd been so naive to think he'd be content so far from other children. He was dependent on us for transportation, which often meant we imposed our presence on other parents who wouldn't have had to see us ever, if we were in a suburb and he could merely skip down the sidewalk. It was a rare friend who would bring a small child to our place and walk through 800 feet of heavy snow before learning whether anyone was there. A telephone would have been nice....

It was a gradual process, our leaving the homestead. In the spring of 1977, I accepted a part-time job in Montpelier and commuted the fifty-five miles each way. In late summer, just as I was realizing the commute would be difficult once the snow arrived, I received a call at work from a friend who knew of a house near Montpelier that needed a caretaker. "Rent free, all you have to do is keep the pipes from freezing," he said. Ben was just a few days from entering first grade, so in haste we made what we thought would be a temporary move. Janet was pregnant, so we were glad for a house with modern conveniences. By the time Anna was born, my job had become full-time. We sold the farmhouse and bought a small place in Ben's school district. Sited on a two-acre lot behind an abandoned farm, it had electricity, running water, and telephone.

When I bought the farm in Enosburg in 1968, Vermont had 5,264 working dairy farms. By 1988, that figure had dropped to 2,525. Ours is one of the 2,739 dairy farms that has been lost. In light of the values that first attracted us to homesteading, in light of the growing public concern about the future of farming and the future of the planet, in light of what was already in motion when Janet and I first left the mainstream of suburban, college-educated junior adults, I think we've given up an important vision of who we might be and how we might contribute, through restraint, to the health of our planet.

But give it up we did, without ever realizing that was what we were doing. Even after we moved into our new house, we had not moved the furniture and other possessions from our cabin. We did not want to acknowledge that our homesteading days were over.

Now every time I purchase and carry home a product wrapped in some nonbiodegradable container, every time I thoughtlessly let a lightbulb burn all day, whenever I buy a truckload of split and delivered maple, I have to admit that within the bubble of a forty-hour week, I've lost touch. Maybe I quit hammering my head too soon. I was probably a source of tragicomic relief to those old-timers who remember when wood stoves, kerosene light, and outhouses were not considered "alternative," but I acquired skills I'd have otherwise never developed, and I came close to acquiring the sense of planning that is essential to practical living.

When we visit the cabin, three or four times a year, the first thing I check is the water, and once a year I help Richard Carr, a good friend and former neighbor, stack wood in return for his help mucking out the spring and sometimes pumping air and mud back up the pipe to get the system running again. This summer I rented a force pump and drove north to meet Richard. We hauled the heavy pump and thirty gallons of water for priming in his van because my little Toyota is ill-suited to country work.

To Hell with the Homestead!   163

Richard and I explore our friendship during these visits, and I'd miss something valuable if the water system didn't require occasional work. I thought about that as I drove home, pleased that we'd restored the flow of water up our hill. I also realized that maintaining the water system, while the cabin falls into disrepair, is symbolic. As far as homesteading goes, the water line was my one identifiable "success" fifteen years earlier.

Looking back and ahead, I see that the challenge is not to live off the land but to live with the land. Having made some marvelous errors, I suspect we'll be prepared if circumstance or choice return us to the simple life. I hope our children have developed a perspective on these alternatives, though I know they can't acquire skills through osmosis: better we were still living the life of homesteaders than reminiscing. But at least now I know how to keep chickens and whether they need to be pregnant to deliver eggs. Why I think I could even build an outhouse with a door! The social pessimist in me says these skills may someday come in handy. Janet and I sometimes talk of moving back to the cabin once Anna and Ben are out on their own.

And what of our washing machine? Early Monday morning I followed the instructions of Dennis Appliance. I never found a sock in the pump, and I inspected the pipe—to no avail—for an obstruction. I called Dennis back. He promised to visit before day's end, which he did, billing me $35.00 for the trip and $9.95 for the belt he replaced. For free he stuck a pair of needle-nosed pliers into the pump, extricating what he'd suspected was there all along, visible, I suppose, only to the experienced eye—the cause of our badly singed belt—a sock.

About the Authors

Lennie Britton

Lennie Britton traces his family roots back to the 1770s in Windsor where he was born. Raised in Woodstock, he graduated from the University of Vermont and Dartmouth College.

A documentary and film writer, one of his screenplays—a historical drama about the first woman to run for president—recently won a development grant from the National Endowment for the Arts. In 1985 he coproduced for WCAX-TV in Burlington "Dilemmas of Development," a series examining Vermont's development problems.

Lennie currently lives with his wife, Jane, on a small farm in North Pomfret. During the winter he works with the Woodstock Ski Runners Educational Foundation, an organization dedicated to keeping the sport of skiing accessible to local children.

Frank Bryan

Frank Bryan's political philosophy finds expression in many ways—as a political science professor at the University of Vermont, as a commentator about local affairs, and as an outspoken critic of the ways of government. Frank is the author of several books including *Yankee Politics in Rural Vermont,* and co-author, with Bill Mares, of *Real Vermonters Don't Milk Goats,* and *OUT!* His most recent book, written with John McLaughry, *The Vermont Papers,* proposes a complete restructuring of Vermont's government.

Frank lives with his family in Starksboro.

Joseph Citro

Referred to alternately as "The Robert Frost of Gore," or "Vermont's answer to Stephen King," Joe Citro has written several horror novels including *The Unseen, Shadow Child*, and *Guardian Angels*. All are heavily dependent on Vermont history and folklore. His soon-to-be released *Dark Twilight* deals with the Lake Champlain monster. In 1989 and 1990, Joe served as treasurer of Horror Writers of America. He is an active member of the League of Vermont Writers.

Rickey Gard Diamond

Expatriate midwesterner, Rickey Gard Diamond has been living and writing in Montpelier since 1980.

In 1985, she was the founding editor of *Vermont Woman*. Her essays and articles have appeared in *Vermont Vanguard, The Times Argus, Creating Excellence*, and *Vermont History*. She is currently working on a series of books for junior-high-age girls.

A fiction writer, too, her short stories have appeared in *The Louisville Review, Kalliope, Plainswoman, Other Voices*, and *The Sewanee Review*.

Geof Hewitt

Geof Hewitt grew up in New Jersey, then attended Cornell University and completed masters programs at Johns Hopkins University and the University of Iowa. He taught for a year at the University of Hawaii before moving to Vermont where he married Janet Lind and began the adventures he describes in these pages.

In 1975, Geof took a motor tour of the United States and interviewed people for a book titled *Working for Yourself*, published by Rodale Press. He also has published two collections of poems, *Stone Soup* (1974) and *Just Worlds* (1989). He has also conducted writers' workshops in colleges and coffeehouses across the country.

Geof currently is the writing/secondary English consultant for the Vermont State Department of Education. He lives in Calais.

Lee Pennock Huntington

Lee Pennock Huntington has served at U.S. embassies in Bogota and Paris, has worked with refugees in Tunisia and Algeria as a member of the American Friends Service Committee during the French-Algerian War, and was a staff member of the Quaker Program at the United Nations directed by her husband, William Reed Huntington.

For sixteen years she was a reviewer for the Book-of-the-Month Club, was the first book editor of *Country Journal*, and since 1971 has been book critic for the *Rutland Herald* and *Vermont Sunday Magazine*.

As critic and trustee of the Vermont Council on the Arts, she has a special interest in Vermont writers. She is the author of six books for children and of *Hill Song*, a journal of her life in Rochester, Vermont, which was a Book-of-the-Month Club selection. She currently lives in Norwich.

Bill Mares

Former State Representative William Mares succinctly writes his autobiography as follows: "I brew my own beer, I run marathons, and I fly fish. I've not won a literary prize since the 9th grade."

For the record, he is also the author of six books including *Working Together, The Marine Machine,* and (with co-author Frank Bryan) *Real Vermonters Don't Milk Goats,* and *OUT!* He lives in Burlington with his wife, Christine Hadsel, and his two sons.

Don Mitchell

Don Mitchell lives with his wife, children, and assorted animals on a farm in Vergennes. He is the author of *Moving UpCountry, Living UpCountry, Thumb Tripping, Fourstroke,* and *The Souls of Lambs.*

His thoughts about country life are a regular feature in the *Boston* magazine column, "RFD." When he's not wrestling sheep, Don teaches writing at Middlebury College.

Howard Norman

Howard Norman's most recent book, *Kiss in the Hotel Joseph Conrad*, is a collection of stories. His first novel, *The Northern Lights*, was nominated for a National Book Award in 1987. He is the editor of *NORTHERN TALES* in the Pantheon Folklore and Fairytale Library.

Presently he teaches in the MFA program at the University of Maryland and lives in East Calais and Washington, D.C. He is adapting his short story, "Laughing and Crying," for public television.

Andy Potok

A gifted painter until he was blinded by a degenerative eye disease, Andy Potok has given up his paints for a pen. His book *Ordinary Daylight* detailed his struggle with encroaching blindness and was chosen in 1980 as a Literary Guild Alternate Selection. His first novel, *My Life with Goya*, was published in 1986.

Andy lives in Plainfield, Vermont, with his wife, Charlotte, and his Seeing Eye dog, Dash.

Norman Runnion

Formerly editor of the *Brattleboro Reformer* for twenty years, Norman Runnion is currently attending seminary. He is a former trustee of the Vermont Historical Society and served on the advisory board of *Vermont Life* magazine from 1984 to 1990.

He was born in Kansas City, Missouri, and worked as a journalist in Europe and Washington, D.C., before moving to Vermont in 1966.

Norma Jane Skjold

Norma Jane Skjold is a journalist with twenty-five years' experience as a staff and free-lance writer for daily newspapers and magazines in New Jersey, Nebraska, and Vermont. She earned an MFA degree in creative writing from Goddard College in 1978 and teaches English composition, journalism, and creative writing part-time for Community College.

Norma has been a staff writer for *The Washington World* in Barre for the last nine years, where she writes the regular column, "With

Due Respect." In her "spare" time, she's at home in South Woodbury writing fiction "that might as well be true."

Tom Slayton

Tom Slayton has been a journalist, writer, and editor for more than twenty-five years. He was a reporter, bureau chief, and editor for the *Rutland Herald* and *Barre-Montpelier Times Argus* from 1964 to 1985. In 1985, he was appointed editor of *Vermont Life* magazine. He has also contributed articles to the *Boston Globe*, the *Miami Herald*, *Natural History* magazine, and other newspapers and magazines.

He is the author of *Finding Vermont*, an informal guide to Vermont's history, land, and people. He is a Bicentennial Fellow of the University of Vermont and teaches writing in the journalism department of St. Michael's College.

He lives in Montpelier with his wife, Elizabeth, and son, Ethan.

Fred Stetson

Fred Stetson grew up by a salt marsh on the north end of Duxbury Bay in Massachussetts but has lived in Vermont for twenty-two years. He is an avid sailor and hiker, is a graduate of Middlebury College, and is a member of the board of directors of the Vermont Folklife Center.

He writes for *Vermont Life* and the *Montreal Gazette* and wrote—with Tom Hill—*Ultralight Boatbuilding*. He lives with his wife, Kate Pond, and daughter, Elizabeth, in Burlington.

Douglas Wilhelm

Douglas Wilhelm was born in Oregon, grew up in New Jersey, spent a summer when he was fifteen working on a dairy farm, and came to live in Vermont in 1983, when he was thirty.

A free-lance writer and editor in Montpelier, he contributed news and feature articles to the *Boston Globe* from 1985 to 1989 and began writing its Sunday "New England Notebook" column in 1986. He lives on Main Street in the capital city.

Alex Wilson

Alex Wilson is a technical and free-lance writer in West Dummerston, Vermont. He writes for both trade and consumer magazines on topics related to building technology, energy, and the environment. He has published more than 100 articles in such magazines as *Custom Builder, The Journal of Light Construction, Architecture, Yankee Homes, Mother Earth News, HomeOwner, Practical Homeowner, Harrowsmith, Independent Energy, Sanctuary,* and *Vermont Business.*

In addition to magazine writing, Alex provides technical writing services for a wide range of corporations and agencies through his company, West River Communications, Inc. Before going out on his own in 1985, he was executive director of the New England Solar Energy Association in Brattleboro.